MW01228374

" The Comprehensive Guide to Agriculture in India for Competitive Exams"

"Empower your competitive exam journey with 'The Comprehensive Guide to Agriculture in India for Competitive Exams,' offering in-depth knowledge and real-world insights from agricultural experts."

Authors
Ravi Yadav, M.Sc. Horticulture (Vegetable Science)
Ravi Shankar Ratre, Horticulture (Vegetable Science)
Dr. V.K. Singh (Professor)

Contant

Contents

Acknowledgments

I am deeply grateful to everyone who has contributed to the creation of the **"Comprehensive Guide to Agriculture in India for Competitive Exams."** This book would not have been possible without the support, guidance, and encouragement of many individuals.

First and foremost, I would like to express my sincere thanks to the agricultural experts and educators who generously shared their knowledge and insights. Their expertise has greatly enriched the content of this guide, ensuring its accuracy and relevance.

I am also thankful to the numerous farmers and agricultural professionals. Their contributions have added invaluable practical insights to the theoretical knowledge presented in this book.

Special go to my colleagues and friend who offered constructive feedback and suggestions during the writing process.

I would like to acknowledge the support of my family, whose patience and understanding have been unwavering thanks throughout this journey. Their encouragement has been a constant source of motivation.

This book is dedicated to all the students preparing for competitive exams in agriculture. I hope it serves as a valuable resource and helps you achieve your academic and professional goals. Thank you.

Ravi Yadav
Ravi Shankar Ratre

Dr. V.K. Singh

Summary

The "Comprehensive Guide to Agriculture in India for Competitive Exams" serves as an exhaustive resource designed to equip exam aspirants with in-depth knowledge of the Indian agricultural sector. The guide is meticulously structured into ten chapters, covering a wide array of topics such as the historical and economic importance of agriculture, agro-climatic zones, soil and water management, crop production techniques, horticulture, livestock, and poultry management, fisheries, agricultural marketing, finance, and insurance, as well as agricultural research and education. Each chapter is divided into detailed s that address specific aspects, from government policies and reforms to technological advancements and future. This guide not only delves into the practicalities of farming but also explores the broader socio-economic impacts, aiming to provide a holistic understanding of Indian agriculture for competitive exam success.

Authors

Ravi Yadav
Ravi Shankar Ratre
Dr. V.K. Singh

A. Some Short Forms for Agriculture-Based Competitive Exams:

1. **ICAR** - Indian Council of Agricultural Research

2. **IBPS-AFO** - Institute of Banking Personnel Selection - Agricultural Field Officer

3. **NABARD** - National Bank for Agriculture and Rural Development

4. **FSSAI** - Food Safety and Standards Authority of India

5. **AIEEA** - All India Entrance Examination for Admission (conducted by ICAR)

6. **JRF/SRF** - Junior Research Fellowship / Senior Research Fellowship (conducted by ICAR)

7. **IARI** - Indian Agricultural Research Institute (entrance exams for postgraduate courses)

8. **UPCATET** - Uttar Pradesh Combined Agriculture and Technology Entrance Test

9. **BHU PET** - Banaras Hindu University Postgraduate Entrance Test (for agriculture courses)

10. **MP PAT** - Madhya Pradesh Pre-Agriculture Test

11. **TS EAMCET-AGRI** - Telangana State Engineering, Agriculture and Medical Common Entrance Test (for agriculture)

12. **AP EAMCET-AGRI** - Andhra Pradesh Engineering, Agriculture and Medical Common Entrance Test (for agriculture)

13. **AGRICET** - Agriculture Common Entrance Test (conducted by Acharya N.G. Ranga Agricultural University for diploma holders)

14. **Rajasthan JET** - Rajasthan Joint Entrance Test for Agriculture

15. **MCAER PG CET** - Maharashtra Council of Agricultural Education and Research Postgraduate Common Entrance Test

16. **CG PAT** - Chhattisgarh Pre-Agriculture Test

17. **KEAM-AGRI** - Kerala Engineering Architecture Medical Entrance Exam (for agriculture courses)

18. **GBPUAT** - Govind Ballabh Pant University of Agriculture and Technology Entrance Exam

19. **ICAR AIEEA PG** - ICAR All India Entrance Examination for Admission for Postgraduate courses

20. **AAU VET** - Assam Agricultural University Veterinary Entrance Test

21. **PAU CET** - Punjab Agricultural University Common Entrance Test

22. **OUAT** - Orissa University of Agriculture and Technology Entrance Exam

23. **BCECE AGRI** - Bihar Combined Entrance Competitive Examination for Agriculture

24. **JET Agriculture** - Joint Entrance Test for Agriculture (various states)

25. **CPAT** - Combined Pre-Agriculture Test (various states)

26. **ICAR NET** - ICAR National Eligibility Test

27. **ASRB ARS** - Agricultural Scientists Recruitment Board Agricultural Research Service

28. **SKUAST** - Sher-e-Kashmir University of Agricultural Sciences and Technology Entrance Exam

29. **RAJUVAS RPVT** - Rajasthan University of Veterinary and Animal Sciences Rajasthan Pre-Veterinary Test

30. **BHU UET-AGRI** - Banaras Hindu University Undergraduate Entrance Test for Agriculture

31. **JCECE AGRI** - Jharkhand Combined Entrance Competitive Examination for Agriculture

32. **AGRI POLYCET** - Agriculture Polytechnic Common Entrance Test (various states)

33. **HORTICET** - Horticulture Common Entrance Test (conducted by Dr. YSR Horticultural University)

34. **TNAU UG/PG** - Tamil Nadu Agricultural University Undergraduate/Postgraduate Entrance Exam

35. **UPCATET** - Uttar Pradesh Combined Agriculture and Technology Entrance Test

36. **ICAR AICE-JRF/SRF** - ICAR All India Competitive Examination for Junior Research Fellowship/Senior Research Fellowship

37. **LUVAS VLDA** - Lala Lajpat Rai University of Veterinary and Animal Sciences Veterinary and Livestock Development Assistant Entrance Exam

38. **CAEPHT** - Central Agricultural University Pre-Entrance Test (for agricultural engineering and technology)

39. **PJTSAU** - Professor Jayashankar Telangana State Agricultural University Entrance Exam

40. **BAU** - Bihar Agricultural University Entrance Exam

41. **UPSC**: Union Public Service Commission

42. **CGPSC**: Chhattisgarh Public Service Commission

43. **MPPSC**: Madhya Pradesh Public Service Commission

B. Important Agricultural Abbreviations with Establishment Dates

1. **ACABC** - Agri-Clinics and Agri-Business Centers Scheme (2002)

2. **AFL** - Agriculture Field Laboratory (Varies by institution, no single establishment date)

3. **AI** - Artificial Insemination (Concept from the early 1900s, widespread use from 1930s)

4. **AIEEA** - All India Entrance Examination for Admission (Conducted by ICAR since 1998)

5. **APEDA** - Agricultural and Processed Food Products Export Development Authority (1985)

6. **APMC** - Agricultural Produce Market Committee (APMC Act - 1963)

7. **ASCI** - Agriculture Skill Council of India (2013)

8. **ATMA** - Agricultural Technology Management Agency (2005)

9. **BCS** - Bio-Control Agents (Concept adopted in the 1970s)

10. **BIS** - Bureau of Indian Standards (1986)

11. **CACP** - Commission for Agricultural Costs and Prices (1965)

12. **CAZRI** - Central Arid Zone Research Institute (1959)

13. **CGIAR** - Consultative Group on International Agricultural Research (1971)

14. **CIMMYT** - International Maize and Wheat Improvement Center (1966)

15. **CRIDA** - Central Research Institute for Dryland Agriculture (1985)

16. **CSIR** - Council of Scientific and Industrial Research (1942)

17. **CSO** - Central Statistical Office (1951, now part of the Ministry of Statistics and Programme Implementation)

18. **CSS** - Centrally Sponsored Scheme (Varies by specific schemes)

19. **DAHD** - Department of Animal Husbandry and Dairying (1919)

20. **DD Kisan** - Doordarshan Kisan (2015, a TV channel dedicated to agriculture)

21. **DGFT** - Directorate General of Foreign Trade (1991)

22. **DRDO** - Defence Research and Development Organisation (1958, includes agricultural research applications)

23. **DRIP** - Drip Irrigation Program (Widespread adoption in India from the 1970s)

24. **FAO** - Food and Agriculture Organization (1945)

25. **FARM** - Farmers' Agricultural Resource Management (Varies, specific programs)

26. **FICCI** - Federation of Indian Chambers of Commerce & Industry (1927)

27. **FPO** - Farmer Producer Organization (2002)

28. **FRP** - Fair and Remunerative Price (Sugarcane - 2009)

29. **FSSAI** - Food Safety and Standards Authority of India (2006)

30. **GDP** - Gross Domestic Product (Concept from 1934)

31. **GIS** - Geographic Information System (Concept from the 1960s, Agricultural application varies)

32. **GM** - Genetically Modified (First GM crop - 1994, widespread agricultural use from 1990s)

33. **HYV** - High-Yielding Variety (Green Revolution era, 1960s in India)

34. **IARI** - Indian Agricultural Research Institute (1905)

35. **ICAR** - Indian Council of Agricultural Research (1929)

36. **ICMR** - Indian Council of Medical Research (1911, relevant for food and agriculture in health context)

37. **ICRISAT** - International Crops Research Institute for the Semi-Arid Tropics (1972)

38. **ICT** - Information and Communication Technology (Adopted in various agricultural applications since the 1990s)

39. **IFFCO** - Indian Farmers Fertilizer Cooperative Limited (1967)

40. **IFPRI** - International Food Policy Research Institute (1975)

41. **IFS** - Integrated Farming System (Adopted since the 1970s)

42. **IRRI** - International Rice Research Institute (1960)

43. **ISRO** - Indian Space Research Organization (1969, agricultural applications varied)

44. **KCC** - Kisan Credit Card (1998)

45. **KVIC** - Khadi and Village Industries Commission (1956)

46. **KVK** - Krishi Vigyan KEndra (1974)

47. **LPG** - Liberalization, Privatization, and Globalization (Economic policy shift in India - 1991)

48. **MIDH** - Mission for Integrated Development of Horticulture (2014)

49. **MIT** - Micro Irrigation Technology (Widespread adoption since the 1970s)

50. **MNCFC** - Mahalanobis National Crop Forecast Centre (2012)

51. **MSP** - Minimum Support Price (1965)

52. **NABARD** - National Bank for Agriculture and Rural Development (1982)

53. **NAIP** - National Agricultural Innovation Project (2006)

54. **NBAIM** - National Bureau of Agriculturally Important Microorganisms (2001)

55. **NBSS** - National Bureau of Soil Survey (1976)

56. **NCS** - National Centre for Sustainable Agriculture (Varies, based on specific programs)

57. **NDRI** - National Dairy Research Institute (1923)

58. **NFSM** - National Food Security Mission (2007)

59. **NGC** - National Green Corps (2001)

60. **NGO** - Non-Governmental Organization (Concept from 1945, after the establishment of the UN)

61. **NGS** - Next Generation Sequencing (First introduced in 2005)

62. **NHB** - National Horticulture Board (1984)

63. **NHB** - National Horticulture Board (1984)

64. **NHM** - National Horticulture Mission (2005)

65. **NICRA** - National Innovations on Climate Resilient Agriculture (2011)

66. **NMOOP** - National Mission on Oilseeds and Oil Palm (2014)

67. **NMSA** - National Mission for Sustainable Agriculture (2014)

68. **NPV** - Net Present Value (Economic concept, broadly adopted in agriculture since the mid-20th century)

69. **NRCPB** - National Research Centre on Plant Biotechnology (1985)

70. **NREGA** - National Rural Employment Guarantee Act (2005, now MGNREGA)

71. **NRLM** - National Rural Livelihood Mission (2011)

72. **NSC** - National Seed Corporation (1963)

73. **NSFM** - National Food Security Mission (2007)

74. **NSS** - National Service Scheme (1969)

75. **NSSO** - National Sample Survey Office (1950)

76. **PDS** - Public Distribution System (1947, with significant reforms in 1997)

77. **PFA** - Prevention of Food Adulteration Act (1954)

78. **PMFBY** - Pradhan Mantri Fasal Bima Yojana (2016)

79. **PMKSY** - Pradhan Mantri Krishi Sinchai Yojana (2015)

80. **PPVFRA** - Protection of Plant Varieties and Farmers' Rights Authority (2001)

81. **RCF** - Rashtriya Chemicals & Fertilizers (1978)

82. **RCGM** - Review Committee on Genetic Manipulation (1989)

83. **RKVY** - Rashtriya Krishi Vikas Yojana (2007)

84. **RKVY-RAFTAAR** - Rashtriya Krishi Vikas Yojana - Remunerative Approaches for Agriculture and Allied Sector Rejuvenation (2017)

85. **SAU** - State Agricultural University (First - GBPUAT, 1960)

86. **SHG** - Self-Help Group (1972)

87. **SHM** - Soil Health Management (Part of NMSA, 2014)

88. **SRI** - System of Rice Intensification (1983, India adoption from the 2000s)

89. **SWOT** - Strengths, Weaknesses, Opportunities, Threats (Concept from 1960s)

90. **TRIFED** - Tribal Cooperative Marketing Development Federation of India (1987)

91. **WTO** - World Trade Organization (1995)

C. Important Vocabulary in Agriculture

A

1. **Abiotic Factors**: Non-living environmental factors such as soil, water, and climate that influence crop growth and agricultural productivity.

2. **Agribusiness**: Commercial agriculture enterprises involved in the production, processing, and distribution of agricultural products.

3. **Agri-tourism**: A form of commercial enterprise that links agricultural production and/or processing with tourism to attract visitors to a farm, ranch, or other agricultural business to entertain and/or educate the visitors.

4. **Agrochemicals**: Chemical products used in agriculture, including pesticides, herbicides, fungicides, and fertilizers, to manage pests and enhance crop growth.

5. **Agro-Climatic Zones**: Regions classified based on climate and agricultural practices, influencing crop suitability and farming techniques.

6. **Agroecology**: The study of ecological processes applied to agricultural production systems, focusing on sustainable farming practices that mimic natural ecosystems.

7. **Agroecosystem**: An ecological system managed and modified by humans for agricultural production, including crops, livestock, soil, and water.

8. **Agroforestry Systems**: Farming systems that combine trees, crops, and/or livestock on the same land, enhancing biodiversity and productivity.

9. **Agroforestry**: Integrating trees and shrubs into agricultural landscapes to enhance biodiversity, improve soil health, and provide additional income sources.

10. **Agroforestry**: The practice of integrating trees and shrubs into agricultural landscapes to enhance biodiversity, improve soil health, and provide additional income sources.

11. **Allelochemicals**: Chemicals produced by plants that influence the growth, survival, and reproduction of other plants, often involved in allelopathy.

12. **Allelopathy**: The chemical inhibition of one plant by another due to the release of toxic substances, affecting crop growth and yield.

13. **Allelopathy**: The suppression of growth of one plant species by another due to the release of toxic substances.

14. **Alluvial Soils**: Fertile soils composed of silt, sand, clay, and organic matter, found in river plains and deltas.

15. **Anhydrous Ammonia**: A nitrogen fertilizer applied as a gas directly into the soil.

16. **Annual Crops**: Crops that complete their life cycle, from germination to the production of seeds, within one year, and then die.

17. **Anthracnose**: A group of fungal diseases affecting plants, causing dark lesions on leaves, stems, flowers, or fruits.

18. **Anthropogenic**: Environmental changes or processes that are caused by human activities, such as deforestation, pollution, and climate change.

19. **Aquaculture**: The cultivation of aquatic organisms such as fish, crustaceans, and seaweed, in controlled environments for commercial purposes.

20. **Aquaponics**: A system that combines conventional aquaculture (raising aquatic animals such as fish) with hydroponics (cultivating plants in water) in a symbiotic environment.

21. **Aquifer**: An underground layer of water-bearing rock or sediment that can store and transmit groundwater, crucial for irrigation in agriculture.

22. **Arable Land**: Land capable of being plowed and used to grow crops.

B

23. **Biochar**: A form of charcoal produced from organic materials (biomass) through pyrolysis, used as a soil amEndment to improve fertility and sequester carbon.

24. **Biocontrol**: The use of natural predators, parasites, or pathogens to manage agricultural pests and reduce reliance on chemical pesticides.

25. **Biodiversity**: The variety of plant and animal life in a particular habitat, essential for ecosystem health and resilience in agricultural systems.

26. **Biodynamic Agriculture**: A method of farming based on the teachings of Rudolf Steiner, which emphasizes holistic development and interrelationships of soil, plants, and animals.

27. **Biodynamic Farming**: A method of farming that treats farms as unified and individual organisms, emphasizing the integration of crops and livestock, recycling of nutrients, and maintenance of soil health through organic practices.

28. **Biofertilizers**: Natural fertilizers containing living microorganisms that enhance soil fertility by fixing atmospheric nitrogen, solubilizing phosphorus, and stimulating plant growth.

29. **Biofuel**: A fuel derived directly from living matter, such as ethanol or biodiesel.

30. **Biogas**: A mixture of gases produced by the breakdown of organic matter in the absence of oxygen, used as a renewable energy source.

31. **Biopesticides**: Pesticides derived from natural materials such as animals, plants, bacteria, and certain minerals, are used to control pests and diseases in an environmentally friendly manner.

32. **Buffer Strip**: Strips of vegetation are planted between fields and water bodies to trap pollutants and prevent soil erosion.

33. **Buffer Zone**: An area of land designated to separate and protect different land uses, such as agricultural fields from natural habitats or residential areas.

C

34. **Carbon Farming**: Agricultural practices aimed at reducing greenhouse gas emissions and increasing carbon sequestration in soils and vegetation.

35. **Carbon Footprint**: The total amount of greenhouse gases emitted by human activities, including agricultural practices, usually measured in carbon dioxide equivalents.

36. **Carbon Sequestration**: The process of capturing and storing atmospheric carbon dioxide in soil, plants, and other carbon sinks to mitigate climate change.

37. **Catch Crop**: A fast-growing crop planted between successive plantings of main crops, often to improve soil fertility, prevent erosion, and suppress weeds.

38. **Certified Organic**: Products that have been grown and processed according to specific standards set by certifying organizations, avoiding synthetic chemicals and GMOs.

39. **Chlorosis**: The yellowing of leaves due to insufficient chlorophyll, often caused by nutrient deficiencies, poor soil drainage, or disease.

40. **Climate Mitigation**: Strategies and practices aimed at reducing the sources or enhancing the sinks of greenhouse gases to combat climate change.

41. **Climate-Smart Agriculture**: An integrated approach to managing landscapes—cropland, livestock, forests, and fisheries—that addresses the interlinked challenges of food security and climate change.

42. **Climatic Zones**: Regions of the world are classified according to their prevailing climate, affecting the types of crops that can be grown.

43. **Cold Chain**: A temperature-controlled supply chain that helps maintain the quality and safety of perishable products from the farm to the consumer.

44. **Commodity Crop**: Crops that are traded on commodity markets, such as wheat, corn, soybeans, and cotton.

45. **Compaction**: The compression of soil particles, often due to heavy machinery or livestock, leads to reduced pore space, poor water infiltration, and root growth inhibition.

46. **Companion Planting**: The practice of growing different plants together for mutual benefit, such as pest control or improved growth.

47. **Companion Planting**: The practice of growing different plants together to enhance growth, protect against pests, and improve crop yields through beneficial interactions.

48. **Composting**: The process of recycling organic waste, such as crop residues and animal manure, into humus-rich soil amendment through aerobic decomposition.

49. **Conservation Agriculture**: A set of soil management practices that minimize soil disturbance, maintain soil cover, and promote crop rotation to enhance soil health and biodiversity.

50. **Cover Crop**: A crop grown primarily to cover the soil, rather than for harvest, to improve soil health, reduce erosion, and manage weeds and pests.

51. **Cover Cropping**: Planting crops primarily to improve soil health, manage soil erosion, enhance water availability, and increase biodiversity.

52. **Cover Crops**: Crops grown primarily to protect and improve soil health rather than for harvest, such as clover, rye, and vetch, which prevent erosion and enhance soil fertility.

53. **Crop Diversification**: The practice of growing a variety of crops on the same farm to reduce risk, improve soil health, and increase biodiversity.

54. **Crop Insurance**: Financial protection for farmers against crop loss or damage due to natural calamities, pests, and diseases, often provided through government schemes like Pradhan Mantri Fasal Bima Yojana (PMFBY).

55. **Crop Residue**: The remains of crops left in the field after harvest, which can be used for soil conservation, improving soil organic matter, and preventing erosion.

56. **Crop Rotation**: The practice of growing different types of crops in succession on the same land to maintain soil fertility and control pests and diseases.

57. **Crop Yield**: The total quantity of crop produced on a given area of land, typically measured in bushels, pounds, or tons per acre/hectare.

58. **Cultural Practices**: Agricultural practices such as crop rotation, planting dates, and pest management to optimize production and minimize environmental impact.

D

59. **Deciduous**: Trees and shrubs that shed their leaves annually, are often used in agroforestry and permaculture for seasonal benefits.

60. **Defoliation**: The loss of leaves from a plant due to natural processes, pests, diseases, or environmental conditions.

61. **Deforestation**: The clearing of forests for agricultural or other purposes, leading to loss of biodiversity and disruption of ecosystems.

62. **Desertification**: The process by which fertile land becomes desert due to drought, deforestation, or inappropriate agricultural practices.

63. **Drip Irrigation**: A micro-irrigation system where water is delivered directly to the root zone of plants through a network of tubes and emitters, conserving water and reducing evaporation.

E

64. **Ecological Intensification**: Enhancing agricultural productivity through the optimal use of ecosystem services, such as pollination and natural pest control, rather than relying on external inputs.

65. **Ecosystem Approach**: A strategy for managing land, water, and living resources that equitably promotes conservation and sustainable use.

66. **Ecosystem Services**: The benefits that humans receive from ecosystems, such as pollination, water purification, climate regulation, and soil fertility.

67. **endemic**: A species or condition regularly found and restricted to a particular geographic area.

68. **Erosion Control**: Practices designed to prevent soil erosion, such as planting cover crops, building terraces, and creating windbreaks.

69. **Evapotranspiration**: The combined process of water evaporation from the soil and transpiration from plants, influencing water management in agriculture.

70. **Fallow Land**: Agricultural land that is left unplanted for one or more growing seasons to restore soil fertility and reduce pest and disease cycles.

71. **Farm Mechanization**: The use of machinery and technology in farming to increase efficiency and reduce labour.

72. **Farmers' Produce Trade and Commerce (Promotion and Facilitation) Act**: A 2020 act that allows farmers to sell their produce outside the designated Agricultural Produce Market Committee (APMC) markets, aiming to create a single national market.

73. **Farming Systems Research (FSR)**: An interdisciplinary approach to improve agricultural production systems, considering the socio-economic context of the farmers.

74. **Farm-to-Table**: A movement that promotes serving local food at restaurants and school cafeterias, acquired directly from the producer.

75. **Field Capacity**: The amount of soil moisture or water content held in the soil after excess water has drained away and the rate of downward movement has decreased.

76. **Food Miles**: The distance food travels from where it is produced to where it is consumed, impacting its environmental footprint.

77. **Food Security**: The state of having reliable access to sufficient, safe, and nutritious food to maintain a healthy and active life.

78. **Food Sovereignty**: The right of people to define their food systems, prioritizing local production and consumption, sustainable farming practices, and equitable access to resources.

G

79. **Genetic Diversity**: The variety of genes within a species, is important for crop resilience and adaptation to changing environmental conditions.

80. **Genetically Modified Organisms (GMOs)**: Organisms whose genetic material has been altered using genetic engineering techniques to introduce desirable traits such as pest resistance or improved nutritional content.

81. **Grafting**: A horticultural technique where tissues from one plant are inserted into those of another so that the two sets of vascular tissues may join, commonly used in fruit tree production.

82. **Green Manure**: Crops are grown specifically to be ploughed back into the soil to improve fertility and organic matter content, such as clover or alfalfa.

83. **Green Revolution**: A period of agricultural transformation in the 1960s and 1970s that introduced high-yielding varieties (HYVs) of seeds, chemical fertilizers, and advanced irrigation techniques to increase food production.

84. **Greenhouse Effect**: The trapping of heat in the Earth's atmosphere by greenhouse gases, leading to global warming and climate change.

85. **Greenhouse Gases (GHGs)**: Gases in the atmosphere, such as carbon dioxide (CO_2), methane (CH_4), and nitrous oxide (N_2O), that trap heat and contribute to global warming.

H

86. **Hardpan**: A dense layer of soil, usually clay, that is impermeable to water and roots, hindering plant growth.

87. **Hedgerow**: A row of shrubs or trees planted along the edges of fields to act as a windbreak, provide habitat for wildlife, and reduce soil erosion.

88. **Herbicide Resistance**: The ability of a plant to survive and reproduce despite the application of an herbicide intended to kill it, often due to genetic modification or natural selection.

89. **High-Yielding Varieties (HYVs)**: Crop varieties developed through selective breeding that produce higher yields under optimal conditions, often used in the context of the Green Revolution.

90. **Hydraulic Fracturing (Fracking)**: A method of extracting underground resources, such as oil or gas, that can impact water availability and quality for agriculture.

91. **Hydroponics**: A method of growing plants without soil, using nutrient-rich water solutions to provide essential nutrients directly to plant roots.

I

92. **Integrated Crop Management (ICM)**: A farming system that combines the best agricultural practices to maintain economic and ecological balance.

93. **Integrated Farming Systems (IFS)**: Combining different agricultural enterprises such as crop production, livestock rearing, and agroforestry to optimize resource use and enhance sustainability.

94. **Integrated Nutrient Management (INM)**: The combined use of chemical fertilizers, organic manures, and biofertilizers to optimize nutrient availability and enhance soil fertility.

95. **Integrated Pest Management (IPM)**: A sustainable approach to managing pests by combining biological, cultural, physical, and chemical tools in a way that minimizes economic, health, and environmental risks.

96. **Integrated Water Management (IWM)**: A holistic approach to managing water resources that considers the entire water cycle, including supply, demand, quality, and environmental impacts.

97. **Intercropping**: The practice of growing two or more crops together in proximity to promote beneficial interactions and optimize the use of resources.

98. **Irrigation Efficiency**: The effectiveness of irrigation methods in delivering water to crops, is critical for conserving water and improving agricultural productivity.

K

99. **Kisan Credit Card (KCC)**: A government scheme that provides farmers with timely access to credit for their agricultural needs, ensuring financial support for various farming activities.

L

100. **Land Tenure**: The rights and arrangements by which land is owned, used, and transferred, affecting agricultural investment and productivity.

101. **Legume**: A type of plant that has symbiotic nitrogen-fixing bacteria in its root nodules, enriching soil fertility. Examples include beans, lentils, and peas.

102. **Livelihood Diversification**: The process by which households build a diverse portfolio of activities and assets to improve their income and reduce vulnerability to shocks.

103. **Livestock Integration**: The practice of integrating animal husbandry with crop production to enhance farm productivity, nutrient cycling, and biodiversity.

M

104. **Marginal Land**: Land that is less suitable for conventional agriculture due to poor soil fertility, water availability, or other factors, often used for alternative crops or conservation.

105. **Microbial Inoculants**: Beneficial microorganisms applied to seeds or soil to enhance plant growth, nutrient uptake, and disease resistance.

106. **Microclimate**: The climate of a small, specific place within a larger area, influenced by factors such as vegetation, water bodies, and human structures.

107. **Micro-Irrigation**: Efficient irrigation systems like drip and sprinkler irrigation that deliver water directly to the plant root zone, reducing water wastage and increasing irrigation efficiency.

108. **Minimum Support Price (MSP)**: A government-fixed price at which it buys crops from farmers, ensuring them a minimum profit for their harvest.

109.   **Monoculture**: The agricultural practice of growing a single crop species over a large area, which can lead to increased vulnerability to pests and diseases.

110.   **Mulch**: A layer of material, such as straw, leaves, or plastic, spread over the soil surface to conserve moisture, suppress weeds, and improve soil health.

M

111.   **Mycorrhiza**: A symbiotic association between fungi and plant roots that enhances nutrient and water uptake.

N

112.   **Nematodes**: Microscopic, worm-like organisms in soil that can be beneficial or harmful to plants.

113.   **Nitrate Leaching**: The process by which nitrogen in the form of nitrate moves through the soil and into groundwater, potentially causing pollution.

114.   **Nitrogen Fixation**: The process by which certain plants, especially legumes, convert atmospheric nitrogen into forms usable by plants, enhancing soil fertility.

115.   **No-Till Farming**: An agricultural practice where the soil is not ploughed, reducing soil erosion and improving soil health by maintaining organic matter and soil structure.

116.   **Nutrient Cycling**: The movement and exchange of organic and inorganic matter back into the production of living matter, essential for maintaining soil fertility.

O

117.   **Organic Certification**: A certification process for producers of organic food and other organic agricultural

products, ensuring they adhere to organic farming standards.

118. **Organic Farming**: Agricultural practices that rely on natural processes and inputs, avoiding synthetic chemicals, to enhance soil fertility and biological diversity.

P

119. **Permaculture Principles**: Guidelines for designing sustainable agricultural systems that mimic natural ecosystems, emphasizing diversity, resilience, and resource conservation.

120. **Permaculture**: A system of agricultural and social design principles that simulate natural ecosystems to create sustainable and self-sufficient agricultural systems.

121. **Pest Management**: The practice of managing pests to minimize damage to crops, which can include chemical, biological, cultural, and physical control methods.

122. **Photosynthesis**: The process by which green plants use sunlight to synthesize nutrients from carbon dioxide and water, producing oxygen as a by-product.

123. **Phytoremediation**: The use of plants to clean up contaminated soil and water, absorbing pollutants through their roots and improving environmental health.

124. **Phytosanitary**: Relating to the health of plants, particularly the prevention and control of pests and diseases through regulations and treatments.

125. **Polyculture**: The practice of growing multiple crop species in the same space, promoting biodiversity, and reducing pest and disease risks.

126. **Poultry Farming**: The raising of domesticated birds such as chickens, ducks, turkeys, and geese for their meat or eggs.

127. **Precision Agriculture**: Farming management based on observing, measuring, and responding to variability in crops using technology such as GPS and remote sensing.

128. **Precision Farming**: A modern farming practice that uses technology such as GPS and remote sensing to monitor and manage field variability in crops, optimizing inputs and improving yields.

R

129. **Rainwater Harvesting**: The collection and storage of rainwater for agricultural use, reducing depEndency on groundwater and other water sources.

130. **Regenerative Agriculture**: Farming practices that restore soil health, increase biodiversity, improve water cycles, and enhance ecosystem resilience through methods such as no-till farming and cover cropping.

131. **Remote Sensing**: The use of satellite or aerial imagery to collect information about the Earth's surface, often used in agriculture for monitoring crop health and land use.

132. **Resilience**: The capacity of agricultural systems to withstand and recover from adverse conditions such as climate change, pests, and diseases.

133. **Rhizosphere**: The region of soil directly influenced by root secretions and associated soil microorganisms, critical for nutrient uptake and plant health.

134. **Riparian Buffer**: Vegetated areas next to water bodies that help shade and partially protect the water from the impact of adjacent land uses.

135. **Rotational Grazing**: The practice of moving livestock between pastures to allow forage plants to recover and maintain healthy pasture ecosystems.

S

136. **Salinization**: The accumulation of salts in soil, often due to improper irrigation practices, which can reduce soil fertility and crop yields.

137. **Silage**: Fermented, high-moisture fodder stored in a silo, bunker, or wrapped bales, used to feed livestock during times when fresh forage is not available.

138. **Silviculture**: The practice of controlling the establishment, growth, composition, and quality of forests to meet diverse needs and values.

139. **Silvopasture**: A form of agroforestry that combines trees, forage plants, and livestock in an integrated system to enhance productivity and sustainability.

140. **Smart Farming**: The use of information technology, robotics, and data analysis to optimize agricultural processes and increase productivity.

141. **Soil Amendment**: Substances added to soil to improve its physical or chemical properties, such as compost, lime, and gypsum.

142. **Soil Conservation**: Techniques to prevent soil erosion and degradation, such as contour ploughing,

terracing, and cover cropping, to maintain soil health and productivity.

143. **Soil Erosion**: The removal of the topsoil layer by natural forces such as wind and water, leading to reduced soil fertility and agricultural productivity.

144. **Soil Health Card Scheme**: A government initiative providing farmers with detailed information about the nutrient status of their soil and recommEndations for soil health improvement.

145. **Soil Organic Matter (SOM)**: The organic component of soil consisting of plant and animal residues at various stages of decomposition, crucial for soil health and fertility.

146. **Soil pH**: A measure of the acidity or alkalinity of soil, affecting nutrient availability and microbial activity.

147. **Soil Profile**: A vertical section of the soil that reveals its layers, or horizons, which differ in physical, chemical, and biological properties.

148. **Stubble Mulching**: Leaving crop residues on the soil surface after harvest to protect against erosion, retain moisture, and enhance soil organic matter.

149. **Subsidy**: Financial assistance provided by the government to reduce the cost of agricultural inputs like fertilizers, seeds, and irrigation, making them more affordable for farmers.

150. **Subsistence Farming**: Small-scale farming focused on producing enough food to meet the needs of the farmer's family, with little surplus for sale.

151. **Sustainable Agriculture**: Farming practices that meet current food needs without compromising the

ability of future generations to meet their needs, focusing on environmental health, economic profitability, and social equity.

152. **Sustainable Intensification**: Increasing agricultural productivity on existing farmland while minimizing environmental impact and preserving resources.

153. **Sustainable Intensification**: Increasing agricultural productivity on existing farmland while minimizing environmental impact and preserving resources for future generations.

154. **Sustainable Livelihoods**: Strategies that provide individuals and communities with the means to generate income and meet their needs without degrading the environment.

T

155. **Terrace Farming**: The practice of creating stepped levels on hilly terrain to reduce soil erosion, and surface runoff, and enhance water retention.

156. **Terrace Farming**: The practice of creating stepped levels on hilly terrain to reduce soil erosion and surface runoff, enhancing water retention and crop yields.

157. **Transgenic Crops**: Crops that have been genetically engineered to express genes from other species, providing traits such as pest resistance or herbicide tolerance.

158. **Transpiration**: The process by which plants release water vapor through their leaves, playing a key role in plant health and the water cycle.

159. **Trellising**: The use of support structures for climbing plants to improve air circulation, sun exposure, and ease of harvest.

160. **Urban Agriculture**: The practice of cultivating, processing, and distributing food in or around urban areas, contributing to food security and sustainability.

V

161. **Value Chain**: The full range of activities required to bring a product from conception through production to delivery to consumers and disposal.

162. **Varietal Resistance**: The inherent ability of certain crop varieties to resist pests, diseases, or environmental stresses, reducing the need for chemical inputs.

163. **Varietal Trials**: Tests conducted to evaluate the performance of different crop varieties under specific conditions to determine their suitability for cultivation.

164. **Vermiculture**: The cultivation of earthworms for use in composting and soil improvement, producing nutrient-rich vermicompost.

165. **Vertical Farming**: The practice of growing crops in vertically stacked layers, often using controlled-environment agriculture technology to optimize resource use.

166. **Vertical Integration**: The combination of two or more stages of production, usually operated by separate companies, under a single management.

W

167. **Water Harvesting**: The collection and storage of rainwater or runoff for agricultural use, enhancing water availability and reducing dependence on groundwater.

168. **Water Use Efficiency (WUE)**: The ratio of crop yield to the amount of water used, emphasizing the

importance of efficient water management in agriculture.

169. **Watershed Development**: The integrated development of a watershed area to improve water availability, soil conservation, and agricultural productivity through community participation and sustainable practices.

170. **Watershed Management**: The process of managing the natural resources within a watershed area to balance environmental, social, and economic needs, including soil and water conservation.

171. **Watershed**: An area of land where all the water that falls in it drains into a common outlet, such as a river, lake, or ocean, critical for water management in agriculture.

172. **Weed Management**: The practice of controlling unwanted plants that compete with crops for nutrients, water, and light.

173. **Wildlife Corridor**: Areas of habitat that connect wildlife populations separated by human activities or structures, facilitating movement and genetic exchange.

174. **Xeriscaping**: Landscaping and gardening techniques that reduce or eliminate the need for irrigation by using drought-resistant plants and efficient water management practices.

175. **Yield Gap**: The difference between the actual crop yield achieved by farmers and the potential yield under optimal conditions, highlighting areas for improvement in agricultural practices.

176. **Yield Potential**: The maximum possible yield that a crop can achieve under optimal conditions, influenced by genetic and environmental factors.

177. **Zero Tillage**: A conservation agriculture practice where crops are planted directly into the residue of previous crops without tilling the soil, reducing soil erosion and improving soil health.

178. **Zero-Budget Natural Farming (ZBNF)**: A farming practice that promotes the natural growth of crops without the use of synthetic fertilizers and pesticides, relying on locally available natural resources.

179. **Zoonotic Diseases**: Diseases that can be transmitted from animals to humans, often associated with livestock farming and wildlife interactions.

180. **Zoonotic Pathogens**: Disease-causing organisms that can be transmitted from animals to humans, often found in agricultural settings with livestock.

D. College and research station

International Agricultural Universities with a Presence in India

1. **International Crops Research Institute for the Semi-Arid Tropics (ICRISAT)** - Patancheru, Hyderabad, Telangana, Established in 1972

2. **International Rice Research Institute (IRRI)** - Collaboration with Indian Agricultural Research Institute (IARI), No specific establishment date for presence in India; IRRI established in 1960

National Agricultural Universities

1. **Acharya N.G. Ranga Agricultural University (ANGRAU)** - Guntur, Andhra Pradesh, Established in 1964

2. **Anand Agricultural University (AAU)** - Anand, Gujarat, Established in 2004

3. **Assam Agricultural University (AAU)** - Jorhat, Assam, Established in 1969

4. **Bidhan Chandra Krishi Viswavidyalaya (BCKV)** - Nadia, West Bengal, Established in 1974

5. **Bihar Agricultural University (BAU)** - Sabour, Bihar, Established in 2010

6. **Central Institute of Fisheries Education (CIFE)** - Mumbai, Maharashtra, Established in 1961

7. **Chaudhary Charan Singh Haryana Agricultural University (CCSHAU)** - Hisar, Haryana, Established in 1970

8. **Chaudhary Sarwan Kumar Himachal Pradesh Krishi Vishvavidyalaya (CSKHPKV)** - Palampur, Himachal Pradesh, Established in 1978

9. **Dr. Panjabrao Deshmukh Krishi Vidyapeeth (PDKV)** - Akola, Maharashtra, Established in 1969

10. **Dr. RajEndra Prasad Central Agricultural University (DRPCAU)** - Pusa, Bihar, Established in 1970 as RajEndra Agricultural University; converted to Central Agricultural University in 2016

11. **G.B. Pant University of Agriculture and Technology (GBPUAT)** - Pantnagar, Uttarakhand, Established in 1960

12. **Indian Agricultural Research Institute (IARI)** - New Delhi, Established in 1905

13. **Indian Veterinary Research Institute (IVRI)** - Bareilly, Uttar Pradesh, Established in 1889

14. **Indira Gandhi Krishi Vishwavidyalaya (IGKV)** - Raipur, Chhattisgarh, Established in 1987

15. **Jawaharlal Nehru Krishi Vishwa Vidyalaya (JNKVV)** - Jabalpur, Madhya Pradesh, Established in 1964

16. **Junagadh Agricultural University (JAU)** - Junagadh, Gujarat, Established in 2004

17. **Kerala Agricultural University (KAU)** - Thrissur, Kerala, Established in 1971

18. **Maharana Pratap University of Agriculture and Technology (MPUAT)** - Udaipur, Rajasthan, Established in 1999

19. **National Dairy Research Institute (NDRI)** - Karnal, Haryana, Established in 1923

20. **Navsari Agricultural University (NAU)** - Navsari, Gujarat, Established in 2004

21. **Orissa University of Agriculture and Technology (OUAT)** - Bhubaneswar, Odisha, Established in 1962

22. **Punjab Agricultural University (PAU)** - Ludhiana, Punjab, Established in 1962

23. **Rajasthan Agricultural University** - Bikaner, Rajasthan, Established in 1987

24. **Sardar Vallabhbhai Patel University of Agriculture and Technology (SVPUAT)** - Meerut, Uttar Pradesh, Established in 2000

25. **Sardarkrushinagar Dantiwada Agricultural University (SDAU)** - Sardarkrushinagar, Gujarat, Established in 1972

26. **Tamil Nadu Agricultural University (TNAU)** - Coimbatore, Tamil Nadu, Established in 1971

27. **University of Agricultural Sciences, Bangalore (UASB)** - Bengaluru, Karnataka, Established in 1964

28. **University of Agricultural Sciences, Dharwad (UASD)** - Dharwad, Karnataka, Established in 1986

29. **University of Horticultural Sciences, Bagalkot** - Bagalkot, Karnataka, Established in 2008

30. **Uttar Banga Krishi Vishwavidyalaya (UBKV)** - Cooch Behar, West Bengal, Established in 2001

Deemed Universities in Agriculture and Horticulture

1. **Dr. Balasaheb Sawant Konkan Krishi Vidyapeeth (DBSKKV)** - Dapoli, Maharashtra, Established in 1972

2. **Sam Higginbottom University of Agriculture, Technology and Sciences (SHUATS)** - Allahabad, Uttar Pradesh, Established as a Deemed University in 2000 (originally founded in 1910)

3. **Sardar Vallabhbhai Patel University of Agriculture and Technology (SVPUAT)** - Meerut, Uttar Pradesh, Established in 2000

4. **Tamil Nadu Veterinary and Animal Sciences University (TANUVAS)** - Chennai, Tamil Nadu, Established as a Deemed University in 1989

5. **Vasantrao Naik Marathwada Krishi Vidyapeeth (VNMKV)** - Parbhani, Maharashtra, Established in 1972

Central Agricultural Universities

1. **Central Agricultural University (CAU)** - Imphal, Manipur, Established in 1993

2. **Dr. RajEndra Prasad Central Agricultural University (DRPCAU)** - Pusa, Bihar, Established as RajEndra Agricultural University in 1970, became a Central Agricultural University in 2016

3. **Indira Gandhi National Tribal University (IGNTU)** - Amarkantak, Madhya Pradesh, Established in 2007, offers agricultural programs

4. **Rani Lakshmi Bai Central Agricultural University (RLBCAU)** - Jhansi, Uttar Pradesh, Established in 2014

Universities with Significant Horticulture Programs

1. **Dr. Y.S. Parmar University of Horticulture and Forestry** - Solan, Himachal Pradesh, Established in 1985

2. **Sri Konda Laxman Telangana State Horticultural University** - Hyderabad, Telangana, Established in 2014

3. **University of Agricultural and Horticultural Sciences, Shimoga** - Shivamogga, Karnataka, Established in 2012

4. **University of Horticultural Sciences, Bagalkot** - Bagalkot, Karnataka, Established in 2008

5. **Y.S.R. Horticultural University** - Venkataramannagudem, Andhra Pradesh, Established in 2007

E. **Important Varieties Based on mostly preferable by farmers in Pan India**

Horticulture

Fruits

1. **Mango**

   o **Alphonso**: Known for its sweetness, richness, and flavor; popular in Maharashtra and Gujarat.

   o **Banganapalli**: Popular in Andhra Pradesh; known for its sweet flavor and firm flesh.

   o **Dasheri**: Originates from Uttar Pradesh; known for its sweet taste and aroma.

   o **Langra**: Popular in Uttar Pradesh and Bihar; known for its distinctive taste.

2. **Banana**

- o **Robusta**: Widely grown in Tamil Nadu and Maharashtra; known for its high yield and disease resistance.

- o **Grand Naine**: Popular across India; known for its good yield and quality.

3. **Apple**

   - o **Red Delicious**: Popular in Himachal Pradesh and Jammu & Kashmir; known for its sweetness and crispness.

   - o **Golden Delicious**: Grown in Himachal Pradesh; known for its sweet taste and firm texture.

4. **Guava**

   - o **Allahabad Safeda**: Known for its white flesh and high vitamin C content; popular in Uttar Pradesh.

   - o **Lucknow 49**: Also known as Sardar; popular in Uttar Pradesh and Maharashtra.

5. **Citrus**

   - o **Nagpur Orange**: Known for its sweet and tangy flavor; popular in Maharashtra.

   - o **Kinnow**: A Mandarin variety popular in Punjab and Rajasthan.

6. **Grapes**

   - o **Thompson Seedless**: Popular in Maharashtra; known for its sweetness and use in raisin production.

   - o **Anab-e-Shahi**: Known for its large size and good flavor; grown in Andhra Pradesh.

7. **Papaya**

- **Red Lady**: Known for its high yield, sweet taste, and disease resistance; popular in Southern India.

- **Pusa Dwarf**: Popular in Northern India; known for its dwarf stature and high fruit production.

8. **Pomegranate**

- **Bhagwa**: Known for its large, sweet fruits and disease resistance; popular in Maharashtra.

- **Ganesh**: Known for its sweet taste and good yield; popular in Maharashtra and Gujarat.

9. **Sapota (Chikoo)**

- **Kalipatti**: Known for its sweetness and high yield; popular in Gujarat and Maharashtra.

- **Pala**: Known for its high yield and good quality; popular in Karnataka.

10. **Pineapple**

- **Kew**: Known for its large size and sweet flavor; popular in Assam and West Bengal.

- **Queen**: Smaller and more aromatic; popular in Meghalaya and Manipur.

11. **Lychee**

- **Shahi**: Known for its high yield and sweet flavor; popular in Bihar.

- **China**: Known for its good fruit size and quality; popular in Bihar and West Bengal.

12. **Jackfruit**

- **Varikka**: Known for its firm and sweet bulbs; popular in Kerala.

- **Panruti**: Known for its high yield and quality; popular in Tamil Nadu.

13. Custard Apple (Sitaphal)

- **Balanagar**: Known for its large fruit size and sweet taste; popular in Andhra Pradesh and Maharashtra.

- **Arka Sahan**: Hybrid variety is known for its good yield and quality; popular in Karnataka.

14. Strawberry

- **Chandler**: Known for its sweet taste and good yield; popular in Himachal Pradesh and Maharashtra.

- **Sweet Charlie**: Known for its early fruiting and disease resistance; popular in Mahabaleshwar, Maharashtra.

15. Litchi

- **Shahi**: Known for its sweet taste and high yield; popular in Bihar.

- **Bombai**: Known for its large size and juicy flesh; popular in West Bengal.

16. Passion Fruit

- **Kaveri**: Hybrid variety is known for its high yield and quality; popular in Kerala and Karnataka.

- **Purple**: Known for its sweet flavor and high yield; popular in North-Eastern states.

Vegetables

1. Tomato

- **Pusa Ruby**: Known for its high yield and disease resistance; popular in Northern India.

- o **Arka Vikas**: Developed by IIHR Bangalore; known for its high yield and good quality.

2. **Brinjal (Eggplant)**

   - o **Pusa Purple Long**: Known for its long, purple fruits and high yield; popular in Northern India.

   - o **Arka Nidhi**: Known for its resistance to bacterial wilt; grown in Karnataka.

3. **Onion**

   - o **Pusa Red**: Known for its high yield and good storage quality; popular in Northern India.

   - o **N-53**: Known for its bulb size and shelf life; popular in Maharashtra.

4. **Cabbage**

   - o **Golden Acre**: Known for its compact head and resistance to black rot; popular in Northern India.

   - o **Pusa Mukta**: Known for its disease resistance and high yield.

5. **Cauliflower**

   - o **Pusa Snowball**: Known for its compact curds and high yield; popular in Northern India.

   - o **Snowball 16**: Known for its good curd quality and resistance to diseases.

6. **Potato**

   - o **Kufri Jyoti**: Known for its high yield and resistance to late blight; popular in Northern India.

   - o **Kufri Pukhraj**: Known for its early maturity and high yield; popular in Uttar Pradesh and Punjab.

7. **Okra (Lady's Finger)**

- **Pusa Sawani**: Known for its high yield and disease resistance; popular in Northern India.
- **Arka Anamika**: Known for its high yield and good quality; popular in Karnataka.

8. **Carrot**

- **Pusa Kesar**: Known for its high yield and good color; popular in Northern India.
- **Nantes**: Known for its sweet flavor and tEnder texture; popular in Karnataka and Maharashtra.

9. **Peas**

- **Arkel**: Known for its early maturity and sweet taste; popular in Northern India.
- **Pusa Pragati**: Known for its high yield and disease resistance; popular in Punjab.

10. **Bitter Gourd**

- **Pusa Vishesh**: Known for its high yield and good quality; popular in Northern India.
- **Preethi**: Known for its high yield and disease resistance; popular in Kerala.

11. **Capsicum (Bell Pepper)**

- **Indra**: Known for its thick flesh and high yield; popular in Karnataka and Himachal Pradesh.
- **California Wonder**: Known for its sweet taste and disease resistance; popular in Tamil Nadu.

12. **Cucumber**

- **Poinsett**: Known for its high yield and resistance to downy mildew; popular in Tamil Nadu and Karnataka.

- o **Pusa Sanyog**: Known for its good quality and yield; popular in Northern India.

13. Bottle Gourd

- o **Pusa Naveen**: Known for its smooth skin and high yield; popular in Northern India.

- o **Arka Bahar**: Known for its uniform size and good quality; popular in Karnataka.

14. Spinach

- o **Pusa Harit**: Known for its high yield and good quality leaves; popular in Northern India.

- o **All Green**: Known for its fast growth and disease resistance; popular in Maharashtra.

Flowers

1. Marigold

- o **Pusa Narangi Gainda**: Known for its bright orange flowers and high yield; popular in Northern India.

- o **Pusa Basanti Gainda**: Known for its yellow flowers and disease resistance; popular in Northern India.

2. Rose

- o **Taj Mahal**: Known for its deep red color and long stems; popular in Maharashtra.

- o **First Red**: Known for its large flowers and good vase life; popular in Tamil Nadu.

Spices

1. Turmeric

- o **Salem**: Known for its high curcumin content; popular in Tamil Nadu.

- **Rajapuri**: Known for its aroma and color; grown in Maharashtra.

2. **Chilli**

   - **Guntur Sannam**: Known for its spiciness; popular in Andhra Pradesh.

   - **Byadagi**: Known for its color and mild pungency; grown in Karnataka.

3. **Black Pepper**

   - **Panniyur 1**: Known for its high yield and disease resistance; popular in Kerala.

   - **Karimunda**: Known for its quality and high yield; popular in Kerala.

4. **Cardamom**

   - **Njallani**: Known for its high yield and large capsules; popular in Kerala.

   - **Green Gold**: Known for its quality and high yield; popular in Kerala.

5. **Coriander**

   - **CO 4**: Known for its high yield and aromatic leaves; popular in Tamil Nadu.

   - **Pant Haritma**: Known for its high yield and disease resistance; popular in Northern India.

6. **Fenugreek**

   - **Pusa Early Bunching**: Known for its early maturity and high yield; popular in Northern India.

   - **Kasuri**: Known for its strong aroma and good quality; popular in Rajasthan and Punjab.

7. **Turmeric**

- o **Erode**: Known for its high curcumin content and bright color; popular in Tamil Nadu.

- o **Duggirala**: Known for its high yield and quality; popular in Andhra Pradesh.

Important Varieties in Agriculture

Cereals

1. **Rice**

   - o **IR64**: Known for its high yield and disease resistance; popular in Andhra Pradesh and Tamil Nadu.

   - o **Sona Masuri**: Known for its aroma and quality; popular in Karnataka and Andhra Pradesh.

   - o **Basmati**: Known for its aroma and long grains; popular in Punjab and Haryana.

2. **Wheat**

   - o **HD 2967**: Known for its high yield and disease resistance; popular in Punjab and Haryana.

   - o **PBW 343**: Known for its high yield and adaptability; popular in Punjab.

3. **Maize**

   - o **Ganga 5**: Known for its high yield and adaptability; popular in Bihar and Uttar Pradesh.

   - o **Dekalb**: Hybrid varieties known for high yield; popular in Karnataka and Maharashtra.

4. **Sorghum**

   - o **CSH 14**: Known for its high yield and drought tolerance; popular in Maharashtra and Karnataka.

- Maldandi: Known for its good quality grain and fodder; popular in Maharashtra.

5. **Barley**

   - **RD 2668**: Known for its high yield and disease resistance; popular in Rajasthan and Haryana.

6. **Finger Millet (Ragi)**

   - **Indaf 9**: Known for its high yield and drought tolerance; popular in Karnataka.

   - **GPU 28**: Known for its high yield and disease resistance; popular in Tamil Nadu.

7. **Pearl Millet (Bajra)**

   - **HHB 67**: Known for its high yield and drought tolerance; popular in Rajasthan and Gujarat.

   - **ICTP 8203**: Known for its high yield and resistance to downy mildew; popular in Maharashtra.

8. **Foxtail Millet (Kangni)**

   - **SIA 3156**: Known for its high yield and adaptability; popular in Karnataka and Andhra Pradesh.

   - **CO 7**: Known for its high yield and short duration; popular in Tamil Nadu.

   - **K 551**: Known for its high yield and quality; popular in Uttar Pradesh

Pulses

1. **Pigeon Pea (Arhar)**

   - **Pusa 992**: Known for its high yield and disease resistance; popular in Uttar Pradesh and Maharashtra.

- **ICPL 88039**: Known for its early maturity and high yield; popular in Karnataka.

2. **Chickpea (Gram)**

   - **Pusa 256**: Known for its high yield and disease resistance; popular in Madhya Pradesh and Rajasthan.

   - **JG 11**: Known for its early maturity and high yield; popular in Andhra Pradesh.

3. **Green Gram (Moong)**

   - **Pusa Vishal**: Known for its high yield and short duration; popular in Northern India.

   - **CO 6**: Known for its high yield and disease resistance; popular in Tamil Nadu.

4. **Black Gram (Urad)**

   - **T 9**: Known for its high yield and early maturity; popular in Uttar Pradesh and Madhya Pradesh.

   - **PDU 1**: Known for its disease resistance and high yield; popular in Tamil Nadu.

Oilseeds

1. **Groundnut**

   - **TMV 2**: Known for its high yield and disease resistance; popular in Tamil Nadu and Karnataka.

   - **GG 20**: Known for its high yield and good quality; popular in Gujarat.

2. **Mustard**

   - **Pusa Bold**: Known for its high yield and disease resistance; popular in Haryana and Rajasthan.

- **Varuna**: Known for its adaptability and high yield; popular in Uttar Pradesh.

3. **Sunflower**

   - **Morden**: Known for its high yield and oil content; popular in Karnataka and Andhra Pradesh.

   - **KBSH 1**: Hybrid variety is known for its high yield; popular in Karnataka.

4. **Soybean**

   - **JS 335**: Known for its high yield and wide adaptability; popular in Madhya Pradesh and Maharashtra.

   - **Pusa 9712**: Known for its high yield and disease resistance; popular in Northern India.

5. **Sesame**

   - **TNV 7**: Known for its high yield and good oil content; popular in Tamil Nadu.

   - **GT 10**: Known for its high yield and disease resistance; popular in Gujarat.

6. **Castor**

   - **GCH 4**: Known for its high yield and resistance to wilt; popular in Gujarat.

   - **Jyothi**: Known for its high yield and adaptability; popular in Andhra Pradesh

7. **Red Gram (Tur)**

   - **BSMR 736**: Known for its high yield and disease resistance; popular in Maharashtra.

   - **Maruti**: Known for its short duration and high yield; popular in Karnataka.

8. **Lentil**

   o **Pusa Masoor 5**: Known for its high yield and disease resistance; popular in Northern India.

   o **Pant L 406**: Known for its high yield and good quality; popular in Uttar Pradesh.

9. **Linseed (Flax)**

   o **Shubhra**: Known for its high yield and oil content; popular in Uttar Pradesh.

   o **Parvati**: Known for its high yield and disease resistance; popular in Madhya Pradesh.

10. **Safflower**

   o **A1**: Known for its high yield and drought tolerance; popular in Maharashtra.

   o **Bhima**: Known for its high yield and oil content; popular in Karnataka.

Fibre Crops

1. **Cotton**

   o **Bt Cotton**: Known for its high yield and resistance to bollworms; popular in Maharashtra, Gujarat, and Andhra Pradesh.

   o **Suraj**: Known for its high yield and quality; popular in Gujarat and Maharashtra.

   o **LRA 5166**: Known for its high yield and resistance to bollworms; popular in Tamil Nadu.

   o **H 777**: Known for its high yield and quality; popular in Gujarat and Maharashtra.

2. **Jute**

- **JRO 524**: Known for its high yield and quality; popular in West Bengal and Assam.

- **JRO 8432**: Known for its high yield and disease resistance; popular in Bihar and Odisha.

- **JRO 8432**: Known for its high yield and disease resistance; popular in Bihar and Odisha.

- **JRC 7447**: Known for its high yield and good quality; popular in West Bengal and Assam.

Classifications

1. Based on Season:

Kharif Crops:

- **Examples:** Rice, Maize, Cotton, Soybean, Groundnut
- **Sowing Season:** Beginning of the monsoon (June to July)
- **Harvesting Season:** End of monsoon (September to October)

Rabi Crops:

- **Examples:** Wheat, Barley, Mustard, Peas, Gram
- **Sowing Season:** Beginning of winter (October to November)
- **Harvesting Season:** End of winter (March to April)

Zaid Crops:

- **Examples:** Watermelon, Muskmelon, Cucumber, Fodder crops
- **Sowing Season:** Between Rabi and Kharif (March to June)
- **Harvesting Season:** Early monsoon (June to July)

2. Based on Lifecycle:

Annual Crops:

- **Examples:** Wheat, Rice, Maize, Mustard

- **Characteristics:** Complete their lifecycle in one growing season.

Biennial Crops:

- **Examples:** Carrot, Beetroot, Onion
- **Characteristics:** Complete their lifecycle in two years, typically vegetative growth in the first year and flowering in the second.

Perennial Crops:

- **Examples:** Sugarcane, Banana, Tea, Coffee
- **Characteristics:** Live for more than two years, producing crops annually once mature.

3. Based on Purpose:

Food Crops:

- **Examples:** Rice, Wheat, Maize, Barley
- **Purpose:** Grown primarily for human consumption.

Forage Crops:

- **Examples:** Alfalfa, Clover, Sorghum
- **Purpose:** Grown to feed livestock.

Fiber Crops:

- **Examples:** Cotton, Jute, Hemp
- **Purpose:** Grown for their fiber to produce textiles and other products.

Oilseed Crops:

- **Examples:** Sunflower, Soybean, Mustard, Groundnut
- **Purpose:** Grown for extracting edible oils.

Cash Crops:

- **Examples:** Coffee, Tea, Rubber, Sugarcane
- **Purpose:** Grown primarily for sale to return a profit.

4. Based on Economic Importance:

Staple Food Crops:

- **Examples:** Rice, Wheat, Maize
- **Characteristics:** Primary source of food for a large population.

Commercial Crops:

- **Examples:** Cotton, Sugarcane, Tobacco
- **Characteristics:** Grown for the purpose of trade and economic gain.

Plantation Crops:

- **Examples:** Tea, Coffee, Rubber, Cocoa
- **Characteristics:** Grown on large estates, typically for export.

5. Based on Botanical Classification:

Cereals:

- **Examples:** Wheat, Rice, Maize, Barley
- **Characteristics:** Grasses cultivated for their edible grains.

Legumes:

- **Examples:** Beans, Peas, Lentils, Chickpeas
- **Characteristics:** Plants with seed pods that split along both sides when ripe.

Tubers:

- **Examples:** Potato, Sweet Potato, Cassava
- **Characteristics:** Plants that produce underground storage organs.

Fruits:

- **Examples:** Apples, Oranges, Bananas, Mangoes
- **Characteristics:** Edible products of a flowering plant.

Vegetables:

- **Examples:** Carrots, Broccoli, Spinach, Tomatoes
- **Characteristics:** Edible parts of plants other than sweet fruits and seeds.

6. Based on Photosynthesis Pathway:

C3 Crops:

- **Examples:** Rice, Wheat, Barley
- **Characteristics:** Use the C3 carbon fixation pathway; common in cooler climates.

C4 Crops:

- **Examples:** Maize, Sugarcane, Sorghum
- **Characteristics:** Use the C4 carbon fixation pathway; efficient in high light and temperature.

CAM Crops:

- **Examples:** Pineapple, Agave
- **Characteristics:** Use Crassulacean Acid Metabolism (CAM) for photosynthesis, suited for arid conditions.

1. Fruit Crops:

Tropical Fruits:

- **Examples:** Mango, Banana, Pineapple, Papaya

- **Characteristics:** Require warm climates and do not tolerate frost.

Subtropical Fruits:

- **Examples:** Citrus (Orange, Lemon), Avocado, Fig
- **Characteristics:** Thrive in regions with mild winters and hot summers.

Temperate Fruits:

- **Examples:** Apple, Pear, Cherry, Plum
- **Characteristics:** Require a period of cold temperatures to break dormancy and produce fruit.

Small Fruits/Berries:

- **Examples:** Strawberry, Raspberry, Blueberry, Gooseberry
- **Characteristics:** Generally grown on small plants or bushes; often rich in vitamins and antioxidants.

2. Vegetable Crops:

Leafy Vegetables:

- **Examples:** Lettuce, Spinach, Kale, Cabbage
- **Characteristics:** Grown for their edible leaves; often high in vitamins and minerals.

Root and Tuber Vegetables:

- **Examples:** Carrot, Beetroot, Potato, Sweet Potato
- **Characteristics:** Grown for their edible underground parts; rich in carbohydrates.

Bulb Vegetables:

- **Examples:** Onion, Garlic, Leek
- **Characteristics:** Grown for their bulbous underground storage organs.

Fruiting Vegetables:

- **Examples:** Tomato, Cucumber, Eggplant, Pepper
- **Characteristics:** Grown for their edible fruits; often require support structures.

Leguminous Vegetables:

- **Examples:** Peas, Beans, Lentils
- **Characteristics:** Grown for their edible pods or seeds; beneficial for soil nitrogen fixation.

Cole Crops:

- **Examples:** Broccoli, Cauliflower, Brussels Sprouts
- **Characteristics:** Belong to the Brassicaceae family; grown for their edible flowers or buds.

3. Ornamental Crops:

Flowering Plants:

- **Examples:** Rose, Tulip, Marigold, Orchid
- **Characteristics:** Grown for their attractive flowers; used for decorative purposes.

Foliage Plants:

- **Examples:** Ferns, Pothos, Calathea
- **Characteristics:** Grown for their attractive leaves; popular in indoor and landscape gardening.

Lawn and Turf Grasses:

- **Examples:** Bermuda Grass, Kentucky Bluegrass, Zoysia
- **Characteristics:** Grown for lawns, sports fields, and ornamental purposes.

4. Tree Crops:

Nut Crops:

- **Examples:** Almond, Walnut, Pecan, Hazelnut
- **Characteristics:** Grown for their edible seeds; often require a long period to mature and produce.

Shade and Ornamental Trees:

- **Examples:** Oak, Maple, Magnolia, Dogwood

- **Characteristics:** Grown for their aesthetic appeal and environmental benefits.

5. Plantation Crops:

Beverage Crops:

- **Examples:** Tea, Coffee, Cocoa
- **Characteristics:** Grown for their leaves, seeds, or beans used to produce beverages.

Spice Crops:

- **Examples:** Black Pepper, Vanilla, Cardamom, Clove
- **Characteristics:** Grown for their flavorful and aromatic components used in cooking and food preservation.

6. Medicinal and Aromatic Plants:

Medicinal Plants:

- **Examples:** Aloe Vera, Neem, Turmeric, Echinacea
- **Characteristics:** Grown for their therapeutic properties and use in traditional and modern medicine.

Aromatic Plants:

- **Examples:** Lavender, Rosemary, Peppermint, Basil

- **Characteristics:** Grown for their fragrant oils and compounds used in perfumes, cosmetics, and aromatherapy.

7. Miscellaneous Crops:

Hydroponic Crops:

- **Examples:** Leafy greens, Herbs, Tomatoes
- **Characteristics:** Grown in nutrient-rich water solutions without soil; suitable for controlled environment agriculture.

Greenhouse Crops:

- **Examples:** Cucumbers, Peppers, Strawberries, Ornamentals
- **Characteristics:** Grown in protected environments to extend growing seasons and control conditions.

Cattle Breeds:

Dairy Breeds:

- **Holstein-Friesian:** Known for high milk production.
- **Jersey:** Produces milk with high butterfat content.
- **Guernsey:** Known for rich, golden milk.
- **Ayrshire:** Adaptable and produces high-quality milk.

Beef Breeds:

- **Angus:** Known for high-quality, marbled beef.
- **Hereford:** Hardy and efficient in feed conversion.
- **Charolais:** Known for their large size and rapid growth.
- **Simmental:** Dual-purpose breed, used for both milk and meat.

Dual-Purpose Breeds:

- **Red Sindhi:** Used for both milk and draught purposes.
- **Sahiwal:** Excellent milk producers and also used for work.

2. Sheep Breeds:

Wool Breeds:

- **Merino:** Known for fine wool quality.
- **Rambouillet:** Produces high-quality wool and good meat.
- **Lincoln:** Produces long, lustrous wool.

Meat Breeds:

- **Suffolk:** Known for rapid growth and high-quality meat.
- **Dorset:** Can breed out of season, providing consistent meat supply.
- **Hampshire:** Produces good quality meat and wool.

Dual-Purpose Breeds:

- **Polypay:** Good for both meat and wool production.
- **Romney:** Known for high-quality wool and meat production.

3. Goat Breeds:

Dairy Breeds:

- **Saanen:** High milk yield and preferred for commercial dairies.
- **Alpine:** Known for good milk production.
- **Nubian:** Produces rich, creamy milk with high butterfat content.

Meat Breeds:

- **Boer:** Known for fast growth and high-quality meat.
- **Kiko:** Hardy breed, known for meat production.
- **Spanish Goat:** Adaptable and used for meat production.

Fiber Breeds:

- **Angora:** Produces mohair.
- **Cashmere:** Known for soft, luxurious cashmere fiber.

4. Poultry Breeds:

Egg-Laying Breeds:

- **Leghorn:** Known for high egg production.

- **Rhode Island Red:** Dual-purpose, good for eggs and meat.
- **Sussex:** Good layers of large eggs.

Meat Breeds:

- **Cornish Cross:** Known for rapid growth and large size.
- **Broilers:** General term for chickens bred for meat production.

Dual-Purpose Breeds:

- **Orpington:** Good layers and provide quality meat.
- **Plymouth Rock:** Reliable layers and good meat producers.

5. Swine Breeds:

Meat Breeds:

- **Yorkshire:** Known for lean meat and good mothering abilities.
- **Duroc:** Known for good growth rate and meat quality.
- **Hampshire:** Known for lean meat and high carcass quality.

6. Equine Breeds:

Light Breeds:

- **Arabian:** Known for endurance and speed.
- **Thoroughbred:** Primarily used in horse racing.

- **Quarter Horse:** Known for versatility and speed over short distances.

Draft Breeds:

- **Clydesdale:** Known for strength and used in heavy farm work.
- **Percheron:** Versatile and used in agriculture and forestry.
- **Shire:** Largest horse breed, used in heavy draft work.

7. Buffalo Breeds:

Dairy Breeds:

- **Murrah:** Known for high milk yield.
- **Nili-Ravi:** Known for high milk production.

Draught Breeds:

- **Surti:** Used for both milk and draught purposes.

8. Camel Breeds:

Riding Breeds:

- **Dromedary (Arabian Camel):** Single-humped, used for riding and racing.

Pack and Draught Breeds:

- **Bactrian (Asian Camel):** Double-humped, used for carrying loads.

9. Rabbit Breeds:

Fur Breeds:

- **Angora:** Known for their wool.
- **Rex:** Valued for their soft fur.

Meat Breeds:

- **New Zealand:** Known for rapid growth and meat quality.
- **Californian:** Good meat yield and growth rate.

1. Freshwater Fish Breeds:

Carp Species:

- **Common Carp (Cyprinus carpio):** Widely cultured for its fast growth and adaptability.
- **Grass Carp (Ctenopharyngodon idella):** Known for feeding on aquatic vegetation.
- **Silver Carp (Hypophthalmichthys molitrix):** Filter feeder, effective in controlling plankton.

Catfish Species:

- **Channel Catfish (Ictalurus punctatus):** Popular in North America for aquaculture.

- **African Catfish (Clarias gariepinus):** Known for fast growth and high adaptability.

Tilapia Species:

- **Nile Tilapia (Oreochromis niloticus):** Highly popular due to rapid growth and good taste.
- **Blue Tilapia (Oreochromis aureus):** Tolerant of a wide range of environmental conditions.

Other Freshwater Species:

- **Trout (Oncorhynchus mykiss):** Preferred for its high-quality meat.
- **Rohu (Labeo rohita):** A significant species in Indian aquaculture.

1. Inland Fisheries:

Freshwater Aquaculture:

Carps:

- **Indian Major Carps:**
  - **Rohu (Labeo rohita):** A major species in Indian aquaculture, known for its high market demand and nutritional value.
  - **Catla (Catla catla):** Known for its fast growth and high yield.

- o **Mrigal (Cirrhinus cirrhosus):** Commonly cultured alongside rohu and catla for its complementary feeding habits.
- **Exotic Carps:**
  - o **Common Carp (Cyprinus carpio):** Widely cultured for its adaptability and fast growth.
  - o **Grass Carp (Ctenopharyngodon idella):** Used for controlling aquatic weeds and also for its meat.
  - o **Silver Carp (Hypophthalmichthys molitrix):** Known for its plankton-feeding habits, often used in polyculture systems.

Catfish:

- **Indian Catfish (Clarias batrachus):** Popular for its taste and adaptability.
- **Pangasius (Pangasianodon hypophthalmus):** Known for its rapid growth and high demand in both domestic and export markets.

Tilapia:

- **Nile Tilapia (Oreochromis niloticus):** Gaining popularity due to its fast growth and high resistance to diseases.

Freshwater Prawns:

- **Giant River Prawn (Macrobrachium rosenbergii):** Cultured for its high market value and export potential.

2. Brackish Water Aquaculture:

Shrimps:

- **Whiteleg Shrimp (Litopenaeus vannamei):** Dominates brackish water aquaculture due to its fast growth, disease resistance, and high export demand.
- **Tiger Shrimp (Penaeus monodon):** Known for its large size and high market value, widely cultured in coastal regions.

Finfish:

- **Asian Seabass (Lates calcarifer):** Popular for its taste and high market demand.
- **Milkfish (Chanos chanos):** Cultured for its adaptability to various salinities and its market demand.

3. Marine Fisheries:

Marine Finfish:

- **Indian Mackerel (Rastrelliger kanagurta):** A significant species for coastal fisheries, known for its high nutritional value.

- **Pomfret (Pampus argenteus):** Valued for its delicate flavor and high market price.
- **Kingfish (Scomberomorus commerson):** Popular for its taste and high commercial value.

Marine Crustaceans:

- **Mud Crab (Scylla serrata):** Cultured for its high market demand and export potential.

Seaweed:

- **Kappaphycus alvarezii:** Cultivated for carrageenan extraction, used in various industries including food, cosmetics, and pharmaceuticals.
- **Gracilaria spp.:** Cultivated for agar production, widely used in food and pharmaceutical industries.

4. Ornamental Fisheries:

Freshwater Ornamental Fish:

- **Goldfish (Carassius auratus):** Popular in the ornamental fish trade.
- **Guppies (Poecilia reticulata):** Known for their vibrant colors and ease of breeding.
- **Betta (Betta splendens):** Valued for their striking colors and finnage.

Marine Ornamental Fish:

- **Clownfish (Amphiprioninae):** Popular in marine aquariums due to their association with sea anemones.
- **Damselfish (Pomacentridae):** Known for their bright colors and active behavior.

5. Integrated Fish Farming:

Rice-Fish Farming:

- **Paddy Cum Fish Culture:** Involves growing fish in paddy fields, enhancing both rice and fish production while utilizing the same land and water resources.

Duck-Fish Farming:

- **Integrated Duck-Fish Farming:** Ducks are raised alongside fish ponds, providing natural fertilization and pest control for the ponds, while ducks benefit from the water habitat.

6. Coldwater Fisheries:

Trout:

- **Rainbow Trout (Oncorhynchus mykiss):** Cultured in hilly regions of India like Himachal Pradesh, Jammu &

Kashmir, and Uttarakhand due to its preference for cold, clear waters.

1. Mulberry Sericulture:

Bombyx mori (Mulberry Silkworm):

- **Characteristics:** The primary silkworm species used in sericulture, feeding exclusively on mulberry leaves.
- **Silk Type:** Produces high-quality Mulberry silk, which is known for its lustrous and fine texture.
- **Regions:** Majorly produced in Karnataka, Andhra Pradesh, Tamil Nadu, West Bengal, and Jammu & Kashmir.

2. Non-Mulberry Sericulture:

Tasar Sericulture:

Tropical Tasar (Antheraea mylitta):

- **Characteristics:** Feeds on leaves of plants like Arjun (Terminalia arjuna) and Asan (Terminalia tomentosa).
- **Silk Type:** Produces coarse, strong, and copper-colored Tasar silk.
- **Regions:** Primarily found in the central and eastern parts of India, including Jharkhand, Chhattisgarh, Odisha, Maharashtra, and West Bengal.

Temperate Tasar (Antheraea proylei):

- **Characteristics:** Hybrid silkworm adapted to cooler climates.
- **Silk Type:** Similar to tropical Tasar but with slightly different texture and quality.
- **Regions:** Found in temperate regions such as Manipur and Meghalaya.

Eri Sericulture:

Eri Silkworm (Samia ricini):

- **Characteristics:** Feeds on castor leaves (Ricinus communis) and can also feed on tapioca and cassava leaves.
- **Silk Type:** Produces Eri silk, known as "Ahimsa silk" or "Peace silk" because the silkworms are not killed in the process. It is soft, warm, and has a woolly feel.
- **Regions:** Primarily produced in Assam, Meghalaya, Nagaland, and other northeastern states.

Muga Sericulture:

Muga Silkworm (Antheraea assamensis):

- **Characteristics:** Feeds on leaves of Som (Machilus bombycina) and Soalu (Litsea polyantha) plants.
- **Silk Type:** Produces golden-yellow Muga silk, known for its durability and natural sheen.

- **Regions:** Exclusive to Assam and some parts of Meghalaya.

3. Oak Tasar Sericulture:

Oak Tasar Silkworm (Antheraea pernyi):

- **Characteristics:** Feeds on oak leaves (Quercus spp.).
- **Silk Type:** Produces strong and coarse silk similar to tropical Tasar but adapted to different climatic conditions.
- **Regions:** Found in the sub-Himalayan belt including Himachal Pradesh, Uttarakhand, Jammu & Kashmir, and some parts of northeastern India.

Classification Summary for Farmers:

- **Mulberry Sericulture:** Focused on Bombyx mori, the most common and economically significant, producing high-quality silk. Suitable regions include Karnataka, Andhra Pradesh, Tamil Nadu, West Bengal, and Jammu & Kashmir.
- **Tasar Sericulture:** Includes Tropical and Temperate Tasar silkworms producing coarse, copper-colored silk, primarily in central and eastern India (Jharkhand, Chhattisgarh, Odisha).
- **Eri Sericulture:** Known for Eri silk, a soft, warm, and ethically produced silk, predominantly in Assam and other northeastern states.

- **Muga Sericulture:** Unique to Assam, producing golden-yellow Muga silk, renowned for its durability and sheen.
- **Oak Tasar Sericulture:** Cultivated in the sub-Himalayan regions, producing strong silk from oak-fed silkworms.

Chapter 1: Introduction to Indian Agriculture

1. 1: Overview of Indian Agriculture

India, a country with vast and diverse landscapes, has a rich history and tradition that is deeply rooted in agriculture. From the fertile plains of the Ganges River to the lush green tea plantations of Assam, agriculture has always been the backbone of India's economy. This sector not only employs a significant part of the population but also ensures the country's food security.

India's agricultural landscape is characterized by a variety of crops, farming practices, and climatic conditions. The country's agricultural economy is divided into several sectors, each specializing in a variety of crops and agricultural activities. These regions have evolved over centuries and are influenced by geography, climate, and socio-economic factors.

Historically, Indian agriculture has undergone many changes. From traditional subsistence farming to the Green Revolution of the 1960s and 1970s, which introduced high-yielding seeds and modern irrigation techniques, the sector has adapted to an ever-changing era. This transformation has enabled India to become one of the largest producers of several crops, including rice, wheat, sugarcane, and cotton.

Despite these advances, Indian agriculture continues to face several challenges. These include monsoon depEndence, fragmentation of land ownership, inadequate infrastructure, and limited access to modern technologies. The Government is committed to addressing these issues through various measures and reforms and promoting sustainable agricultural practices.

The importance of agriculture in India cannot be denied. It contributes about 17-18% of the country's gross domestic product (GDP) and employs about 50% of the workforce. The region is crucial for rural development and provides livelihoods for millions of farmers and their families. In addition, agriculture plays an important role in the socio-economic development of the country, influencing various aspects of rural life, from education and health to social cohesion and cultural heritage.

Indian agriculture is also a major player in the global market. The country is a major exporter of many agricultural products, including spices, tea, coffee, and rice. These exports not only contribute to the national economy but also strengthen India's position in the global agricultural market.

In end, agriculture in India is a complex and dynamic sector that has a profound impact on the country's economy and society. It is a sector that has developed over centuries and remains the cornerstone of India's development. By delving deeper into the different facets of Indian agriculture in this book, we will explore its rich history, current status, and prospects, while providing a comprehensive understanding of this important sector.

1.2: Historical Perspective

The history of Indian agriculture can be traced back to the Indus Valley Civilization (c. 3300-1300 BC), one of the oldest and most advanced civilizations in the world. The people of the Indus Valley developed sophisticated farming techniques, including irrigation systems, crop rotation, and the use of the plow. These innovations laid the foundation for agricultural practices that have evolved over thousands of years.

During antiquity and the Middle Ages, agriculture remained the main occupation of the majority of the Indian population. Agriculture was mainly based on subsistence farming, with farmers growing crops for their own consumption and local trade. The main crops included rice, wheat, barley, lentils, and various fruits and vegetables. The cultivation of spices such as pepper, cardamom, and turmeric also flourished and became an integral part of India's trade with other civilizations.

The advent of the Mughal Empire in the sixteenth century brought significant changes to Indian agriculture. The Mughals introduced new crops such as tobacco, corn, and potatoes, and increased irrigation techniques that increased agricultural productivity. The establishment of large estates and the introduction of land tax systems further shaped the agricultural landscape.

Colonial rule under the British Empire had a profound impact on Indian agriculture. The British introduced commercial agriculture focused on cash crops such as cotton, jute, tea, and indigo, which were exported to Britain to meet the demands of the Industrial Revolution. This shift from subsistence to commercial farming has disrupted traditional farming practices and has had long-term socio-economic consequences.

The post-indepEndence era marked a new phase in Indian agriculture. Faced with food shortages and a growing population, the Indian government launched the Green Revolution in the 1960s. Under Swaminathan's leadership, the Green Revolution aimed to achieve self-sufficiency in food production through the introduction of high-yielding seeds (HYVs), chemical fertilizers, pesticides, and modern irrigation methods.

The Green Revolution brought significant benefits, including higher agricultural yields and improved food security. However, it has also brought challenges such as soil erosion, groundwater depletion, and increased reliance on chemical inputs. These issues have led to a re-evaluation of agricultural practices, with an increasing focus on sustainable and organic farming.

In recent decades, technological advancements have further transformed Indian agriculture. The introduction of biotechnology, precision agriculture, and digital tools has enabled farmers to increase their productivity, manage their resources more efficiently and access market information. Government initiatives such as Pradhan Mantri Fasal Bima Yojana (Fasal Bima Yojana) and

Pradhan Mantri Krishi Sinchai Yojana (Sinchai Yojana) aim to support farmers and address the challenges of the agricultural sector.

Today, Indian agriculture is a mix of traditional practices and modern innovations. It remains an important sector that contributes to the country's economy and provides livelihoods for millions of people. As we move forward, it is important to learn from the past and adopt sustainable practices to ensure the long-term viability of agriculture in India.

1. 3: Importance in the economy

Agriculture is the cornerstone of India's economy and plays an important role in the country's socio-economic development. The sector not only contributes significantly to the gross domestic product (GDP) but is also the main source of income for a large part of the population. Understanding the importance of agriculture to the Indian economy requires a multidimensional approach that takes into account its impact on employment, rural development, and food security.

Contribution to GDP: Agriculture, along with its related sectors, contributes about 17-18% of India's GDP. While this percentage has declined over the years due to the growth of the industrial and service sectors, agriculture remains an important part of the economy. The indirect contribution of the sector through the supply chain, agribusiness, and trade is also important, highlighting its importance for the macroeconomic framework.

Job creation: Agriculture is the main source of employment in India, accounting for about 50% of the total workforce. This is particularly important in rural areas where agricultural activities dominate the employment landscape. The backbone of this workforce is smallholder and smallholder farmers who cultivate small plots of land and contribute to local and national food production.

Rural development: The development of rural areas is closely linked to the performance of the agricultural sector. Improving farm productivity and incomes can lead to improved living standards, education, and health care in rural communities. Government initiatives such as the Mahatma Gandhi National Rural Employment Guarantee Act (MGNREGA) aim to create jobs, improve rural infrastructure, and further support agricultural growth.

Food security: Agriculture is important to ensure food security in India. Since the Green Revolution, the country has made significant progress in food self-sufficiency. India is now one of the largest producers of staple foods such as rice and wheat, as well as other important products such as pulses, fruits, and vegetables. This self-sufficiency makes it possible to stabilize food prices, reduce depEndence on imports, and meet the nutritional needs of the population.

Export potential: India's agricultural sector also plays an important role in international trade. The country is a major exporter of many agricultural products, including rice, spices, tea, and cotton. These exports contribute to the national economy, generate foreign exchange, and strengthen India's position in the global market. Government measures to promote agricultural exports, such as the 2018 Agricultural Export Policy, aim to increase the sector's export potential.

Economic resilience: Agriculture provides a buffer against economic shocks and recessions. In times of economic instability or recession, the agricultural sector often stagnates, providing a safety net for the economy. This flexibility is essential to maintain overall economic stability and support recovery efforts.

Social and cultural importance: Beyond its economic contribution, agriculture in India has immense social and cultural significance. Agricultural methods, festivals, and traditions are closely linked to agricultural activities. Festivals such as Pongal, Baisakhi, and Onam focus on the harvest season and reflect the cultural importance of agriculture in Indian society.

In short, agriculture is the cornerstone of India's economy and underpins various aspects of socio-economic development. Their contribution to GDP, employment, rural development, food security, and international trade underlines their important role. As India continues to grow and develop, it will be crucial to support and develop the agricultural sector to achieve broader economic and social goals.

1. 4: Agricultural Policy and Reforms

Agricultural policy and reforms in India have evolved significantly in recent years, driven by the need to address the challenges of the sector and promote sustainable development. These measures aim to improve productivity, ensure food security, increase farmers' incomes, and make agriculture more resilient to climate and economic shocks.

Agrarian reforms: Agrarian reforms were one of the first initiatives taken after indepEndence to address the distorted distribution of land. The main objective of these reforms was to abolish the zamindari system, redistribute land to farmers, and pass land restriction laws to prevent the concentration of land in the hands of a few. These reforms aim to create a more equitable land tenure structure that will improve agricultural productivity and rural livelihoods.

Green Revolution: The Green Revolution of the 1960s marked a turning point in Indian agriculture. This movement introduced high-yielding seeds (HYVs), chemical fertilizers, pesticides, and advanced irrigation techniques. The states of Punjab, Haryana, and Uttar Pradesh were the main beneficiaries, with a significant increase in crop yields, especially for wheat and rice. While the Green Revolution ensured food security and reduced depEndence on food imports, it also led to problems such as soil erosion, water scarcity, and increased regional inequalities.

Recent land reforms: In recent years, the Indian government has implemented several reforms aimed at liberalizing the agricultural sector and improving farmers' incomes. Key enhancements include:

1. **Agricultural Laws of 2020:**
   - Agricultural Trade and Commerce (Promotion and Facilitation) Act: The Act aims to create an ecosystem where farmers and traders have freedom of choice in the sale and purchase of agricultural products. It allows for the creation of a "one nation, one market" for agricultural products and facilitates interstate trade.
   - Farmers' Agricultural Services and Price Assurance Agreement (Empowerment and Protection) Act: This law provides a framework for contract farming where farmers can enter into agreements with buyers (such as agribusinesses, processors, wholesalers, exporters, or large retailers) before producing or growing agricultural products.
   - Essential Raw Materials (AmEndment) Act: The Act removes raw materials such as cereals, pulses,

oilseeds, edible oils, onions, and potatoes from the list of essential raw materials, thereby regulating their production, storage, circulation, and distribution.

These reforms aim to increase farmers' incomes by giving them more freedom and opportunities to sell their products, ensuring better prices, and attracting private investment in agriculture.

Grant and Support Programs: The Indian government offers various subsidies and support programs to help farmers. These include fertilizers, seeds, subsidies for electricity, and irrigation. Key support plans include:

- **Pradhan Mantri Fasal Bima Yojana (PMFBY):** A crop insurance scheme to provide financial assistance to farmers in the event of crop failures due to natural disasters, pests, and diseases.
- **Pradhan Mantri Krishi Sinchai Yojana (PMKSY):** The objective is to improve irrigation coverage and improve water use efficiency by promoting micro-irrigation techniques.
- **Soil Health Map System:** Provides farmers with information on the nutritional status of their soil and recommEndations for the correct dosage of fertilizers.

Sustainable Agricultural Policy: In response to the environmental challenges posed by intensive agricultural practices, the government promotes sustainable agriculture. Policies and initiatives include:

- **National Mission for Sustainable Agriculture (NMSA):** Focuses on climate-resilient agricultural practices, soil health management, and water efficiency.
- **Organic Farming:** Paramparagat Krishi Vikas Yojana (PKVY) promotes organic farming and financially supports farmers in adopting organic practices.
- **Conservation agriculture:** Promotes practices such as no-till farming, crop rotation, and cover crops to improve soil health and reduce carbon footprint.

Technology and innovation: The introduction of technology and innovation is crucial for the modernization of Indian agriculture. Government initiatives include:

- **Digital agriculture:** The use of digital tools such as mobile apps, electronic marketplaces, and satellite imagery to improve decision-making and market access.
- **Biotechnology:** Developing genetically modified (GM) crops for higher yields and pest resistance, although this remains a controversial topic due to environmental and safety concerns.

After all, agricultural policy and reforms in India have contributed significantly to the transformation of the sector. While significant progress has been made, continued efforts are needed to address new challenges and ensure that agriculture remains a sustainable and profitable activity for farmers.

1.5: Current situation and challenges

Today, Indian agriculture is at a crossroads that reflects the complex interplay of tradition and modernity. Although the sector has made remarkable progress in terms of production and productivity, it continues to face significant challenges that must be addressed to ensure sustainable and inclusive growth.

Current situation: India's agriculture is highly diverse, including a wide range of crops, livestock, and fisheries. Key statistics provide an overview of the current state:

- **Agricultural production:** India is the second largest producer of rice, wheat, and sugar cane, and a major producer of pulses, fruit, and vegetables. The country also occupies an important place in the production of spices, tea, and coffee.
- **Livestock:** India has the largest cattle herd in the world and is a major producer of milk and dairy products. Poultry and fishing also contribute significantly to agriculture.
- **Technology Adoption: Modern** agricultural technologies such as precision agriculture, drip irrigation, and the use of biotechnology are gradually being adopted. Digital platforms are increasingly being used for market access and information dissemination.

- **Infrastructure development:** Rural infrastructure, including roads, storage facilities, and cold chains, has improved, helping to reduce post-harvest losses and improve access to markets.

Challenges: Despite this progress, Indian agriculture continues to face several pressing challenges:

1. **Monsoon depEndence:**
    o A significant portion of India's agriculture depEnds on monsoon rains, making it vulnerable to weather uncertainties. Erratic rainfall and prolonged drought can severely affect crop yields and farmers' incomes.

2. **Fragmented land holdings:**
    o Land fragmentation is a major problem, as the average size of farms is less than two hectares. This limits the possibilities of applying modern agricultural techniques and achieving economies of scale.

3. **Insufficient infrastructure:**
    o Despite improvements, rural infrastructure remains inadequate. Poor road connections, lack of storage facilities, and limited access to electricity and water hamper agricultural productivity and access to markets.

4. **Restricted access to credit:**

- Smallholders and smallholder farmers often have difficulty obtaining formal loans. The reliance on informal lEnders who charge exorbitant interest rates contributes to their financial problems.

5. **Market inefficiencies:**
   - Agricultural markets in India are characterized by long supply chains and inefficiencies with multiple intermediaries. Due to poor market integration and a lack of bargaining power, farmers often receive only a small fraction of the final consumer price.

6. **Soil erosion and water scarcity:**
   - Intensive agricultural practices, excessive use of chemical fertilizers, and poor water management have led to soil erosion and water scarcity. These problems threaten the long-term sustainability of agriculture.

7. **Climate change:**
   - Climate change is a significant threat to Indian agriculture. Rising temperatures, changes in rainfall patterns, and the increasing frequency of extreme weather events can negatively impact crop yields and livestock health.

8. **Low productivity:**
   - The productivity level of many crops in India is lower than the world average. This is due to factors such as outdated agricultural practices, a lack of

high-quality inputs, and the limited use of modern technologies.

9. **Pesticide abuse:**
   o Over-reliance on chemical pesticides has led to the development of pollution, health risks, and pest resistance. Integrated pest management (IPM) practices are not widespread.

10. **Policy and Regulatory Challenges:**
    o Frequent policy changes and regulatory barriers create uncertainty for farmers and agribusinesses. Effective policy implementation and rapid dissemination of information are crucial for the development of this sector.

Growth opportunities: Despite these challenges, there are many opportunities for transformation in Indian agriculture:

- **Sustainable agricultural practices:** Promoting sustainable agricultural practices such as organic farming, conservation agriculture, and agroforestry can increase productivity while protecting the environment.
- **Technological innovation:** Leveraging advances in biotechnology, precision agriculture, and digital agriculture can improve efficiency and productivity.
- **Value creation and agricultural processing: The** development of value-added products and the expansion of

the agri-food industry can create additional sources of income for farmers.

- **Improved market linkages:** Strengthening market linkages through e-marketplace platforms, farmer-producer organizations, and direct sales can ensure better prices for farmers.

- **Capacity building and training:** Providing training and capacity building programs to farmers can improve their skills and knowledge and enable them to adopt modern farming practices.

Policy reforms: Implementing and maintaining farmer-friEndly policies, improving access to credit, and establishing an effective legal framework can create an enabling environment for agricultural growth.

Chapter 2: Agroclimatic Regions of India

2. 1: Definition and classification

India, with its vast geographical extent and diverse climatic conditions, is divided into several agro-climatic zones. These regions are classified based on factors such as temperature, rainfall, soil type, and topography. Understanding these areas is important for the planning and implementation of agricultural strategies, as it helps to identify appropriate crops and farming methods for different regions.

Definition of agroclimatic zones: Agroclimatic zones are geographical regions that have similar climatic conditions and affect the types of crops that can be grown and the agricultural practices that can be applied. These zones are identified based on a variety of parameters, including temperature range, precipitation patterns, humidity, soil type, and elevation.

The concept of agro-climatic zones makes it possible to optimize the use of resources, increase crop productivity, and ensure sustainable agricultural development. By adapting farming practices to the specific conditions of each region, farmers can achieve higher yields and reduce the risk of crop failures.

Classification of agroclimatic zones in India: India is divided into 15 major agroclimatic zones identified by the Planning Commission. These regions are divided into agroecological subregions according to more specific local conditions. The main agroclimatic zones in India are:

1. **Western Himalayan Region:**
   - These include Jammu and Kashmir, Himachal Pradesh, and Uttarakhand.
   - Characterized by mountainous terrain, cold climate, and various soil types.
2. **Eastern Himalayan Region:**
   - Arunachal Pradesh, Sikkim, Assam, Meghalaya, Nagaland, Manipur, Mizoram and Tripura.
   - There is heavy rainfall, hilly terrain, and rich biodiversity.
3. **Lower Ganges Plain:**
   - It includes parts of West Bengal and Bihar.
   - Known for its fertile alluvial soils, high rainfall, and various cultivation methods.
4. **Map of the Middle Ganges:**
   - Covers parts of Uttar Pradesh and Bihar.
   - Characterized by fertile plains, moderate rainfall, and intensive agriculture.
5. **Upper Ganges Plain:**
   - It includes parts of Uttar Pradesh and Uttarakhand.
   - There are fertile alluvial soils, moderate to high rainfall, and diverse cropping systems.
6. **Trans-Ganges Levels:**

- o It includes Punjab, Haryana, Delhi, and parts of Rajasthan.
- o Known for its extensive irrigation, high agricultural productivity, and semi-arid climate.

7. **Eastern Plateau and Mountainous Regions:**
   - o These include Chhattisgarh, Odisha, and parts of Maharashtra.
   - o Hilly terrain, red, lateritic soil, and moderate rainfall can be observed.

8. **Central plateau and mountainous region:**
   - o These include Madhya Pradesh, Uttar Pradesh, and parts of Rajasthan and Maharashtra.
   - o Characterized by black soil, moderate rainfall, and diversified cultivation patterns.

9. **Western Plateau and Hills Region:**
   - o Covers parts of Maharashtra, Madhya Pradesh, and Karnataka.
   - o Black soil, semi-arid climate, and rainfed agriculture.

10. **Southern plateau and mountainous region:**
    - o These include parts of Andhra Pradesh, Karnataka, Tamil Nadu, and Kerala.
    - o It has diverse soils, moderate to high rainfall, and varied topography.

11. **East Coast Plains and Mountainous Regions:**

- o It includes parts of Odisha, Andhra Pradesh, Tamil Nadu, and Pondicherry.
- o Characterized by coastal plains, alluvial soils and heavy rainfall.

12. **West Coast Plains and Ferries:**
   - o It includes parts of Maharashtra, Goa, Karnataka, Kerala, and Tamil Nadu.
   - o Known for its high rainfall, lateritic soils, and diversified cultivation methods.

13. **Plains and hilly regions of Gujarat:**
   - o It includes parts of Gujarat and Rajasthan.
   - o It is characterized by a dry and semi-arid climate, saline soils, and limited rainfall.

14. **Western dry zone:**
   - o It includes parts of Rajasthan.
   - o Characterized by a dry climate, sandy soils, and sparse vegetation.

15. **Island area:**
   - o It includes the Andaman and Nicobar Islands and Lakshadweep.
   - o It is characterized by a tropical climate, high rainfall, and diverse ecosystems.

Importance of agroclimatic zoning: Agroclimatic zoning is essential for effective agricultural planning and management. It helps to:

- **Plant Selection:** Identify the most appropriate plants for each region based on climatic and soil conditions.
- **Resource management:** Optimizing the use of water, fertilizers, and other inputs to increase productivity.
- **Risk reduction:** Reduce the risk of crop failures by introducing region-specific farming practices.
- **Sustainable agriculture:** Promoting sustainable agricultural practices adapted to the local environment.

Finally, it is important to understand India's agroclimatic zones to develop region-specific agricultural strategies. By taking advantage of the unique characteristics of each region, farmers can improve crop yields, increase resource use efficiency, and achieve sustainable agricultural development.

2. 2: Characteristics of each zone

1. Western Himalayan Region:

- **Geography:** The region includes the states of Jammu and Kashmir, Himachal Pradesh, and Uttarakhand. It is a rugged mountainous terrain that stretches from 300 meters above sea level to over 6,000 meters.
- **Climate:** The climate varies from subtropical in the lower valleys to temperate, alpine, and cold desert conditions at high altitudes. A lot of snow falls in the area in winter.

- **The soils** in this region are diverse, including alluvial soils in the valleys, brown mountain soils at intermediate elevations, and podsolic soils at higher elevations.
- **Crops: The** main crops include rice, wheat, corn, barley, apples, plums, and various vegetables. Horticulture, especially apple cultivation, is widespread in the region.
- **Challenges:** The region faces challenges such as soil erosion, landslides, and limited agricultural land due to steep slopes.

2. Eastern Himalayan Region:

- **Geography:** The region includes Arunachal Pradesh, Sikkim, Assam, Meghalaya, Nagaland, Manipur, Mizoram, and Tripura. It is characterized by hilly, mountainous terrain with dense forests.
- **Climate:** The region receives heavy rainfall, especially during the monsoon season, with annual rainfall of more than 1,500 mm to more than 4,000 mm. The climate is tropical to subtropical.
- **Soil:** Soils are generally acidic and have a high organic matter content. Alluvial soils are found in river valleys, while mountain soils dominate in the upper regions.
- **Crops:** Rice, maize, millet, tea, and various fruits and vegetables are the main crops. Tea plantations are particularly important in Assam and Tripura.

- **Challenges:** Soil acidity, shifting cultivation (jhum), and deforestation are the region's biggest challenges.

3. Lower level of the Ganges:

- **Geography:** The region includes parts of West Bengal and Bihar and is characterized by the fertile plains of the Ganges.
- **Climate:** The climate is tropical and humid with heavy rainfall and mild winters during the monsoon season.
- **Soil:** It dominates alluvial soils, known for their fertility and suitability for different crops.
- **Crops:** The most important crops are rice, jute, sugar cane, and various fruits and vegetables. The area is also known for its fishing.
- **Challenges:** Flooding during the monsoon season and soil salinity in some areas are major challenges.

4. Map of the Middle Ganges:

- **Geography:** This region includes parts of Uttar Pradesh and Bihar. It consists of fertile plains with extensive river systems.
- **Climate:** The climate is subhumid, with different summer and winter seasons and moderate to heavy rainfall.
- **Soil:** The nutrient-rich alluvial soil makes this area very productive.

- **Crops:** Rice, wheat, sugarcane, pulses, and oilseeds are the main crops. The region makes a significant contribution to Indian grain production.
- **Challenges: Issues** include waterlogging, soil erosion, and high population density, which put pressure on land resources.

5. Upper Ganges Level:

- **Geography:** The region includes parts of Uttar Pradesh and Uttarakhand and has flat land with fertile soil.
- **Climate:** The climate is subtropical, with hot summers, cold winters, and moderate rainfall.
- **Soil:** Mainly alluvial, deep and fertile soils.
- **Crops: The** main crops are wheat, rice, sugarcane, and pulses. Horticulture and dairy farming are also important.
- **Challenges:** Water scarcity in some areas and the need for sustainable water management practices.

6. Trans-Ganges Levels:

- The region, which includes parts of Punjab, Haryana, Delhi, and Rajasthan, is known for its flat, fertile plains.
- **Climate:** Semi-arid to sub-humid climate with hot summers and mild winters. The region receives moderate rainfall.
- **Soil:** Alluvial land with high fertility, particularly suitable for intensive agriculture.

- **Crops:** Wheat, rice, maize, and cotton are the main crops. This sector makes an important contribution to Indian cereal production.
- **Challenges:** Excessive groundwater extraction, leading to depletion and salinity issues.

7. Eastern Plateau and Hill Regions:

- **Geography:** The region includes parts of Chhattisgarh, Odisha, and Maharashtra, which are characterized by hilly terrain and hills.
- **Climate:** The climate is tropical with variable rainy and dry seasons and moderate to heavy rainfall.
- **Soil:** Red and lateritic soil that is moderately fertile but subject to erosion.
- **Crops:** rice, bajra, pulses, oilseeds and cotton. Forestry and horticulture are also important.
- **Challenges:** soil erosion, deforestation, and limited irrigation options.

8. Middle plateau and mountainous region:

- **Geography:** The region includes Madhya Pradesh, Uttar Pradesh, and parts of Rajasthan and Maharashtra, and consists of plateaus and hill ranges.
- **Climate:** The climate is tropical to subtropical, with hot summers, cold winters, and moderate rainfall.

- **Soil:** Black soil (Regur) and red soil dominate, suitable for cotton, soybeans and legumes.
- **Crops:** Cotton, soybeans, wheat, pulses, and oilseeds are the most important crops.
- **Challenges:** Soil erosion and water scarcity are significant issues.

9. Western Plateau and Mountainous Regions:

- **Geography:** Includes parts of Maharashtra, Madhya Pradesh, and Karnataka that are characterized by rolling terrain and plateaus.
- **Climate:** Semi-arid climate with low to moderate rainfall and high temperatures.
- **Soil:** Mostly black, fertile, moisture-retaining soil.
- **Crops:** cotton, bajra, pulses, oilseeds and sugar cane.
- **Challenges:** water scarcity and drought conditions.

10. Southern Plateau and Hills Region: - Geography: It includes parts of Andhra Pradesh, Karnataka, Tamil Nadu, and Kerala. It has a varied topography with plateaus, hills, and valleys. - **Climate:** Tropical climate with moderate to heavy rainfall and warm temperatures. - **Soil:** Varied soils, including black, red, and lateritic soils. - **Crops:** Rice, millet, pulses, sugarcane, groundnuts, and cotton. Gardening is also important. - **Challenges:** soil erosion, water management, and preservation of soil fertility.

11. East Coast Plains and Hilly Regions: - Geography: Includes Odisha, Andhra Pradesh, Tamil Nadu, and parts of Pondicherry. Characteristic of coastal plains and hills. - **Climate:** Tropical climate with high humidity and heavy rainfall during the monsoon. - **Soil:** Alluvial and coastal soils, suitable for various crops. - **Crops:** Rice, sugar cane, legumes, groundnuts, and fruits. Fishing is also important. - **Challenges:** cyclones, soil salinization, and coastal erosion.

12. West Coast Plains and Ghat Regions: - Geography: It includes parts of Maharashtra, Goa, Karnataka, Kerala, and Tamil Nadu. Known for its coastal plains and the Western Ghats. - **Climate:** tropical climate with high rainfall, and high humidity. - **Soil:** lateritic, fertile and well-drained soil. - **Crops:** rice, coconut, spices, gum and cashews. The cultivation of cultures is important. - **Challenges:** soil erosion, deforestation, and water management.

13. Gujarat Plains and Hill Regions: - Geography: Covers parts of Gujarat and Rajasthan. Characterized by plains, hills, and coastal areas. - **Climate:** Dry to semi-arid climate with low rainfall. - **Soil:** Saline and alkaline soils with some alluvial soils in the river valleys. - Crops: cotton, groundnuts, sesame and millet. Horticulture and dairy farming are important. - **Challenges:** water scarcity, soil salinization, and desertification.

14. Western Dry Zone: - Geography: Includes parts of Rajasthan. Characterized by a dry climate and desert terrain. -

Climate: Extremely dry with very little rainfall and high temperatures. - **Soil:** Sandy soil with low fertility. - **Crops:** Bajra, legumes and oilseeds. Livestock farming is important. - **Challenges:** Water scarcity, desertification, and harsh climatic conditions.

15. Island Region:- Geography: Includes the Andaman and Nicobar Islands, as well as Lakshadweep. Characterized by tropical islands with diverse ecosystems. - **Climate:** Tropical climate with high rainfall and high humidity. - **Soil:** Varied soils, including sandy and alluvial soils. - Crops: Coconut, areca nut, spices and tropical fruits. Fishing is also important. - **Challenges:** Limited arable land, soil salinization, and vulnerability to natural disasters.

Understanding the characteristics of each agro-climatic zone is essential for developing tailor-made agricultural strategies that can optimize productivity and sustainability. By recognizing the unique circumstances and challenges of each region, policymakers and farmers can implement more efficient and sustainable agricultural practices.

2.3: Main crops in each region

Understanding the main crops grown in each agroclimatic zone is key to optimizing agricultural practices, ensuring food security, and increasing farmers' incomes. Each region, with its unique climate and soil conditions, is home to specific plants that thrive in these environments.

1. Western Himalayan Region:

- **Main crops:** rice, maize, wheat, barley, apples, plums, peaches, pears and various vegetables.
- **Highlights:** The area is famous for its apple orchards, especially in Himachal Pradesh. Rice and maize are the main crops grown in the lower valleys, while barley and wheat are prevalent in the higher altitudes.

2. Eastern Himalayan Region:

- **Main crops:** rice, maize, millet, tea, ginger, turmeric, citrus, pineapple, banana and cardamom.
- **Highlights:** Assam is famous for its tea plantations, while Sikkim and the northeastern states grow a variety of horticultural crops such as ginger and turmeric.

3. Lower level of the Ganges:

- **Main crops**: rice, jute, sugar cane, pulses, wheat, potatoes and mangoes.
- **Highlights:** The region is a major producer of rice and jute. West Bengal is known for its high-quality mangoes and extensive jute cultivation.

4. Map of the Middle Ganges:

- **Main crops:** rice, wheat, sugar cane, pulses, maize, and oilseeds.
- **Highlights:** The region is a significant contributor to India's cereal production, particularly rice and wheat. Sugarcane is also an important source of income.

5. Upper Ganges Level:

- **Main crops:** wheat, rice, sugar cane, pulses, oilseeds, and vegetables.
- **Highlights:** The region is known for its high agricultural productivity and produces significant quantities of wheat and sugar cane.

6. Trans-Ganges Levels:

- **Main crops:** wheat, rice, maize, cotton, sugar cane, and oilseeds.
- **Highlights:** Punjab and Haryana are known as the "breadbasket of India" due to their high wheat and rice production. Cotton is also an important crop in the region.

7. Eastern Plateau and Hill Regions:

- **Main crops:** rice, bajra, pulses, oilseeds, cotton and vegetables.

- **Strengths:** The region supports various rice farming models. Millet and legumes are also important, especially in the tribal areas.

8. Middle plateau and mountainous region:

- **Main crops:** cotton, soybeans, wheat, pulses, oilseeds, and sugar cane.
- **Highlights: Black** soils (Regur) are ideal for growing cotton. Soybeans and pulses are also important crops in the region.

9. Western Plateau and Mountainous Regions:

- **Main crops:** cotton, bajra, pulses, oilseeds, sugar cane, and peanuts.
- **Highlights:** The region is known for its cotton and sugarcane production, but it also supports various cropping systems, including pulses and oilseeds.

10. Southern Plateau and Hilly Region: - Main crops: rice, bajra, pulses, sugar cane, groundnut, cotton, and coffee. - **Highlights:** The region is diversified in its agricultural production, with rice being a staple food. Karnataka is known for its coffee plantations and Tamil Nadu for sugar cane and peanuts.

11. East Coast Plains and Hilly Regions: - Main crops: rice, sugarcane, pulses, peanuts, coconut, and banana. - **Highlights:**

Coastal areas support extensive rice cultivation. Andhra Pradesh and Tamil Nadu are major producers of rice and groundnuts.

12. West Coast Plains and Ghat Areas: - Main crops: rice, coconut, spices (pepper, cardamom), gum, cashews, and coffee. - **Highlights:** Kerala is known for its spice and rubber plantations, while the coastal regions support rice and coconut cultivation.

13. Gujarat Plains and Hilly Regions: - Major crops: cotton, groundnut, sesame, millet, and castor. - **Highlights:** Gujarat is a major producer of cotton and groundnuts. Millet and oilseeds are also grown on a large scale in this region.

14. Western Dry Zone: - Main crops: Bajra (millet), pulses, oilseeds, and forage crops. - **Highlights:** This dry region mainly grows drought-tolerant crops such as millet. Livestock farming is also important.

15. Island Region: - Main crops: coconut, areca nut, spices (cloves, nutmeg), tropical fruits (banana, papaya), and vegetables. - **Highlights:** The islands support tropical agriculture with coconut and areca nuts. The climate is conducive to a variety of spices and fruits.

Impact on agricultural practices: The diversity of agro-climatic zones in India requires agricultural practices adapted to each region. By understanding the specific conditions and crop suitability of each region, farmers can adapt their practices, improve yields, and increase sustainability. It also helps to plan agricultural policies and programs that respond more effectively to regional and local challenges.

2.4: Climatic Requirements for Principal Crops

Understanding the climatic requirements of major crops is essential for optimizing agricultural productivity. Each crop has specific requirements in terms of temperature, rainfall, and growing season. Here, we look at the climate requirements of some of the major crops grown in different agroclimatic zones of India.

1. Rice:

- **Temperature:** Optimal growth takes place at temperatures between 20°C and 35°C. At least 10 °C is required for germination.
- **Precipitation:** 1,000 to 2,000 mm of annual precipitation is required. It is usually grown in areas that are very humid and abundant in water.
- **Growing season:** The Kharif season (June to November) is the peak period for rice cultivation. In some areas, rice is also grown during the rabi season (December to April).

2. Wheat:

- **Temperature:** Cold temperatures are necessary for growth, ideally between 12°C and 25°C. Temperatures above 25°C during the grain filling period can reduce yield.
- **Precipitation:** Moderate precipitation of 500 to 1,000 mm is preferred. Excessive rainfall or waterlogging can affect the harvest.
- **Growing season:** Rabi season (October to April), with sowing in October-November and harvesting in March-April.

3. Corn (corn):

- **Temperature:** Grows best in temperatures between 21°C and 27°C. Temperatures below 10°C and above 35°C are harmful.
- **Precipitation:** 500 to 800 mm of precipitation is required. Adequate water supply is important during flowering and grain filling.
- **Growing season:** Can be grown during the Kharif (June to October) and Rabi (November to March) seasons.

4. Sugarcane:

- **Temperature:** Optimal growth takes place at temperatures between 20°C and 35°C. Frost can severely damage the crop.
- **Precipitation:** 750 to 1,200 mm of annual precipitation is required. In areas with low rainfall, irrigation is necessary.

- **Growing season:** Planting times vary by region, usually in February-March and September-October. Their long growth period is 10 to 18 months.

5. Cotton:

- **Temperature:** The ideal temperature for growth is between 21°C and 30°C. Temperatures above 35°C can stress plants.
- **Precipitation:** 600 to 1,200 mm of precipitation is required. Excessive moisture or drought can affect yield.
- **Growing season:** Kharif season (June to November), with sowing in April-June and harvesting in October-January.

6. Legumes (e.g., chickpeas, lentils, pigeon pate):

- **Temperature:** The optimal ascent occurs at temperatures between 18°C and 30°C. Legumes generally tolerate high temperatures, but cold conditions are necessary for the formation of flowers and pods.
- **Precipitation:** 400 to 700 mm of precipitation is required. They are generally drought-tolerant and can grow in semi-arid conditions.
- **Growing season:** Kharif (June to October) and Rabi (October to April), depEnding on the type of legume.

7. Oilseeds (for example, peanut, sunflower, mustard):

- **Temperature:** Peanuts grow best between 25°C and 30°C, sunflowers between 20°C and 30°C and mustard between 10°C and 25°C.
- **Rainfall:** Groundnuts require 500 to 1,000 mm of rainfall, sunflower 600 to 1,000 mm, and mustard 400 to 500 mm.
- **Growing season:** Peanuts are mainly grown during the Kharif season, sunflowers can be grown during the Kharif and Rabi seasons, and mustard is mainly a Rabi plant.

8. Bajra (e.g. Bajra, Jowar, Ragi):

- **Temperature:** Optimal elevation occurs at temperatures between 25°C and 32°C.   Millet is heat tolerant and can withstand high temperatures.
- **Precipitation:** 400 to 600 mm of precipitation is required. They are drought-tolerant and suitable for dry and semi-arid regions.
- **Growing season:** Grown mainly during the Kharif season (June to October), with a few varieties grown during the Rabi season.

9. Horticultural crops (for example, fruits and vegetables):

- **Temperature:** Varies greatly depEnding on the crop. Apples, for example, need cool temperatures (15°C to 25°C), while bananas thrive in warm conditions (20°C to 30°C).

- **Precipitation:** Also varies by crop. For example, citrus fruits require moderate rainfall (750 to 1,200 mm), while grapes require less (500 to 700 mm).
- **Growing season:** varies greatly. Some fruits, such as mangoes, are seasonal (March to June), while vegetables can have multiple growth cycles throughout the year.

10. Spices (e.g., black pepper, cardamom, turmeric):

- **Temperature:** Black pepper and cardamom require moderate temperatures (15°C to 25°C), while turmeric grows well in hot conditions (20°C to 30°C).
- **Precipitation:** Heavy rainfall (1,500 to 2,500 mm) is required for pepper and cardamom. Turmeric requires 1,000 to 2,000 mm of precipitation.
- **Growing season:** Typically grown during the monsoon season (June to September) for black pepper and cardamom, and during the post-monsoon season (October to December) for turmeric.

Adaptable to climatic conditions: To optimize agricultural production, farmers must adapt their practices to the specific climatic conditions of their region. This includes choosing the right plant varieties, timing of planting and harvesting, and implementing irrigation and soil management practices that are appropriate for the local climate. By adapting farming practices to the climatic requirements of crops, farmers can improve yields, reduce risks, and ensure sustainable agriculture.

2.5: Effects of climate change on agriculture

Climate change is a significant threat to agriculture in India, with profound implications for food security, farmers' livelihoods, and the wider economy. The diversity of the country's agro-climatic zones makes it particularly vulnerable to the effects of climate change, which can manifest itself in various forms such as temperature fluctuations, changes in rainfall patterns, and increased frequency of extreme weather events. It is important to understand and address these impacts to develop resilient agricultural practices and strategies.

1. **Temperature rise** :
   - **Impact**: Rising temperatures can affect plant growth and productivity. Heat stress during critical growth phases can reduce yields and quality.
   - **Example**: High temperatures during wheat flowering and grain filling can reduce grain size and reduce yields. Similarly, crops such as rice and maize are sensitive to temperature increases, which can shorten the growing season and affect overall productivity.
2. **Changes in precipitation patterns** :

- Impacts: Changes in the timing, intensity, and distribution of rainfall can disrupt agricultural cycles and lead to droughts or floods.
- For example, delaying the onset of the monsoon can affect the planting of kharif crops such as rice and cotton, while excessive rainfall can cause waterlogging and damage to the crop. In areas depEndent on rain-fed agriculture, erratic rainfall can severely affect crop yields.

3. **Increased frequency of extreme weather events** :
- Impact: Extreme weather events such as hurricanes, floods, and droughts can cause immediate and severe damage to crops, livestock, and infrastructure.
- Example: Cyclones in coastal areas can devastate plantations and fisheries, while floods can destroy crops and erode soils. On the other hand, drought can lead to water shortages, which affects irrigation and livestock.

4. **Soil erosion and desertification** :
- Impacts: Climate change can exacerbate soil erosion by increasing erosion, salinity, and loss of organic matter while reducing soil fertility.
- For example, in semi-arid regions such as Rajasthan, rising temperatures and low rainfall can accelerate desertification and make land less

suitable for agriculture. Soil erosion from intense rainfall can erode topsoil, which is essential for plant growth.

5. **Water shortage:**
   - **Impacts**: Changes in rainfall patterns and increased evaporation rates can lead to water scarcity, impacting irrigation and drinking water supplies.
   - **Example**: Areas depEndent on glacier-fed rivers such as the Indus and Ganges are threatened by melting glaciers, which can initially increase water flow but ultimately reduce water availability. Groundwater depletion due to overexploitation and low recharge rates is also a major challenge.

6. **Spread of pests and diseases** :
   - **Impact**: Warmer temperatures and changes in humidity can create favorable conditions for pests and diseases, which can increase crop losses.
   - **For example**, the spread of pests such as Fall armyworm, which thrives in warmer climates, can damage corn and other crops. Fungal diseases such as rust and downy mildew can also spread as a result of changed weather conditions and affect crops such as wheat and potatoes.

7. **Effects on livestock** :

- o **Impacts**: Climate change can affect livestock through heat stress, reduced feed availability, and increased prevalence of disease.
- o **Example**: Heat stress can reduce milk production in dairy cows and affect reproduction. Changes in feed quality and availability due to changes in rainfall patterns can affect animal nutrition and health.

Optimization Strategies

A variety of adaptation strategies can be used to mitigate the effects of climate change on agriculture:

1. **Diversification of crops and cultivation methods** :
   - o **Strategy:** Farmers can diversify their crops and adopt mixed farming practices to reduce the risk of total crop failure. Growing drought and heat-resistant plant varieties can also increase resilience.
   - o **Examples**: Mixed millet and legume cultivation or the introduction of agroforestry practices that integrate trees with crops and livestock can provide multiple sources of income and improve ecosystem services.
2. **Better water management** :
   - o **Strategy**: Effective water management practices such as rainwater harvesting, micro-irrigation (drip and sprinkler systems), and watershed management

can help conserve water and improve its use efficiency.

- o **Example**: Setting up dams and agricultural ponds to collect rainwater can increase groundwater recharge and provide irrigation during dry periods. Using drip irrigation for high-value crops such as vegetables and fruits can reduce water waste and improve yields.

3. **Soil protection techniques** :
   - o **Strategy**: Practices such as contour tillage, cover cropping, and the use of organic mulch can prevent soil erosion, increase soil fertility, and improve water retention.
   - o **Example**: Growing cover crops such as clover or rye in the off-season can protect the soil from erosion and add organic matter. Mulching with crop residues can preserve soil moisture and suppress weeds.

4. **Climate-resilient infrastructure** :
   - o **Strategy**: The development of climate-resilient infrastructure, such as weatherproof warehouses, improved country roads, and flexible livestock barns, can reduce vulnerability to extreme weather events.
   - o **Example**: Building advanced grain warehouses can protect products from flood damage. Building

livestock cyclone shelters can reduce losses during extreme weather events.

5. **Early warning system and insurance**:
   o **Strategy:** Implementing early warning systems for extreme weather events and expanding crop and livestock insurance can help farmers recover and prepare for the effects of climate change.

   o **Example**: By using mobile weather forecasting services to inform farmers promptly, they can take preventive measures. Crop insurance schemes such as Pradhan Mantri Fasal Bima Yojana (PMFBY) can provide financial assistance in the event of crop failures.

6. **Research and development** :
   o **Strategy**: Investing in research and development to develop climate-resilient plant varieties and innovative agricultural practices can increase the resilience of agriculture.

   o **Example**: The development and propagation of high-yielding, drought-tolerant, and pest-resistant plant varieties by agricultural research institutes can provide farmers with better opportunities to combat climate change.

7. **Political and institutional support** :
   o **Strategy:** Governments and institutions can play an important role in supporting climate-resilient

agriculture through policies, grants, and advisory services.

- o **Examples**: Policies that promote sustainable agricultural practices, provide subsidies for the adoption of climate-resilient technologies, and strengthen agricultural extension services can help farmers adapt to climate change.

End

Addressing the impacts of climate change on agriculture in India requires a multi-pronged approach that integrates scientific research, technological innovation, policy support, and community participation. By implementing adaptation strategies and building resilience, India can ensure the sustainability and productivity of its agricultural sector in the face of climate change.

Chapter 3: Soil and Water Management

3.1: Types of soils in India

India's diverse geography results in different soil types, each with unique characteristics that significantly influence agricultural practices. Understanding these soil types is important for effective soil management and agricultural production.

1. **Alluvial soils:**
    - o **Characteristics**: Rich in minerals and nutrients, alluvial soils are generally fertile and suitable for a variety of crops. They are made up of silt, sand, clay, and organic matter.
    - o **Distribution**: Found mainly in the Indo-Gange plains, coastal areas and river deltas.
    - o **Crops**: Ideal for rice, wheat, sugarcane, and other grains and legumes.
2. **Black Earth (Regur):**
    - o **Properties**: Known for its high moisture retention capacity and its richness in calcium carbonate, magnesium, potash, and lime. They swell and become sticky when wet and burst when dry.
    - o **Distribution**: Found mainly on the Deccan Plateau, including parts of Maharashtra, Madhya Pradesh, Gujarat, Andhra Pradesh, and Tamil Nadu.

- Crops: Best suited for cotton, hence the name "black cotton flooring." Other suitable crops include soybeans, sorghum, and groundnuts.

3. **Red Earth** :
   - **Characteristics**: Red color due to the presence of iron oxides. These soils are generally low in nitrogen, phosphorus, and organic matter, but rich in potash.
   - **Distribution**: Widely distributed in southern and eastern India, including Tamil Nadu, Karnataka, Andhra Pradesh, Odisha and Chhattisgarh.
   - **Crops**: Suitable for growing legumes, millet, groundnuts, and fruit trees.

4. **Lateritic soil** :
   - **Characteristics**: Formed in conditions of high temperatures and heavy rainfall with optional rainy and dry periods. They are rich in iron and aluminum, but low in nitrogen, potash, and organic matter.
   - **Distribution**: Found in the hilly regions of Karnataka, Kerala, Tamil Nadu, Madhya Pradesh, and the northeastern states.
   - **Crops**: Suitable for tea, coffee, cashews, and other plantation crops.

5. **Desert Soil** :

- o **Characteristics:** Sand gravel, poor in organic matter and alkaline in nature. These soils have low moisture retention and are poor in nutrients.
- o **Distribution**: Found mainly in the arid regions of Rajasthan, Gujarat, and parts of Haryana and Punjab.
- o **Crops**: Suitable for drought-tolerant crops such as millet, barley, and legumes.

6. **Montaner Boden** :
   - o **Characteristics**: vary greatly depEnding on altitude and vegetation. In general, these soils are acidic, rich in humus, but poor in potash and phosphorus.
   - o **Distribution**: Found in the hilly regions of Jammu and Kashmir, Himachal Pradesh, Uttarakhand, Sikkim, and Arunachal Pradesh.
   - o **Crops**: Suitable for gardening, including fruits such as apples, pears, and plums, as well as teas and spices.

3. 2: Soil protection techniques

Soil protection is essential to maintain soil health, prevent erosion, and ensure sustainable agricultural productivity. Various techniques have been developed to protect and improve soil quality, each adapting to different types of land and agricultural practices. Here we explore some of the main soil protection techniques used in India.

1. **Tillage in contour lines** :
   - ○ **Technique**: Tillage with the contours of the soil instead of ups and downs.
   - ○ **Benefits**: This method reduces soil erosion by creating a natural barrier that slows water runoff and promotes water intrusion.
   - ○ **Challenges**: Requires careful planning and implementation, which can be tedious.
2. **Terrace:**
   - ○ **Technique**: Create steep bleacher levels to reduce soil erosion and surface runoff.
   - ○ **Benefits**: Roofs slow down the flow of water, allowing more water to penetrate the soil and reducing erosion. This technique is particularly useful in mountainous areas.
   - ○ **Challenges**: Building and maintaining roofs can be expensive and labor-intensive.
3. **Crop rotation** :
   - ○ **Technique**: Growing a variety of crops one after the other on the same land.
   - ○ **Benefits**: Helps maintain soil fertility, reduces pest and disease cycles, and improves soil structure. Crop rotation can increase biodiversity and reduce the need for chemical fertilizers.

- **Challenges**: Requires careful planning and knowledge of plant compatibility and crop rotation cycles.

4. **Cover crop culture** :
   - **Technique**: Plant cover crops such as legumes, hay, or clover in the off-season when the main crops are not being grown.
   - **Benefits: Cover** crops protect the soil from erosion, improve soil organic matter, fix nitrogen, and suppress weeds. They also help retain soil moisture.
   - **Challenges**: Additional costs and labor for growing and managing cover crops. It is important to choose appropriate cover crops to maximize profits.

5. **Agroforestry** :
   - **Technology**: Integration of trees and shrubs into the agricultural landscape.
   - **Benefits**: Trees and shrubs help prevent soil erosion, improve soil structure, increase biodiversity, and generate additional income from wood and non-wood products. Agroforestry systems can also increase water storage and provide habitat for wildlife.
   - **Challenges**: Requires long-term planning and management. Initial installation can be expensive and farmers need to be trained in agroforestry practices.

6. **Mulberry** :
   - ○ **Technique**: Apply a layer of organic or inorganic matter to the soil surface.
   - ○ **Benefits**: Mulching helps retain soil moisture, reduce soil temperature fluctuations, suppress weeds, and add organic matter to the soil as it decomposes. It also protects the soil from erosion.
   - ○ **Challenges**: Requires a steady supply of mulch and regular application. Inorganic mulch may need to be removed or replaced regularly.

7. **Strip Cutting**:
   - ○ **Technique**: Plants in strips that alternate with the contours of the land.
   - ○ **Benefits**: Reduces erosion by creating a physical barrier that slows water runoff and traps soil particles. It also increases biodiversity and can improve pest control.
   - ○ **Challenges**: Careful planning of harvest strips is required to ensure compatibility and maximize profits.

8. **Gentle tillage** :
   - ○ **Technique**: Reduction of the frequency and intensity of tillage.
   - ○ **Benefits**: Conservation tillage improves soil structure, increases organic matter, reduces erosion,

and promotes water infiltration. It also reduces fuel and labor costs.

- o **Challenges**: The transition from traditional tillage to conservation tillage may require new equipment and management practices. Weed control can be difficult in the early stages.

Case Studies of Successful Soil Conservation Efforts in India

- **Case Study 1: Contour Seeding in the Western Ghats** :
  - o Farmers in the Western Ghats have successfully introduced contour tillage to combat soil erosion on steep slopes. This practice has increased water retention, reduced soil losses, and improved crop yields.
- **Case Study 2: Stairs in Himachal Pradesh** :
  - o In the hilly regions of Himachal Pradesh, terraced lines are widely used for vertical land management. This technique has significantly reduced soil erosion and increased arable land, thus increasing agricultural productivity.
- **Case Study 3: Agroforestry in Karnataka** :
  - o Karnataka has seen successful integration of the agroforestry system, where farmers grow trees in addition to crops. This practice has improved soil health, increased biodiversity, and generated

additional income through wood and fruit production.

The application of these soil protection techniques is important for maintaining agricultural productivity and protecting the environment. By using the right methods, farmers can ensure the long-term health and fertility of their soils, contributing to a more resilient and sustainable farming system.

3. 3: Irrigation Methods and Water Management

Effective irrigation methods and water management practices are important to ensure agricultural productivity, especially in areas with variable rainfall. India, with its diverse agro-climatic zones, uses a range of conventional and modern irrigation techniques to optimize water consumption and increase crop yields.

1. **Surface irrigation** :
    o **Technique**: Water is applied by gravity and distributed over the surface of the soil. Common methods include irrigating troughs, basins, and border strips.
    o **Advantages**: Surface irrigation is simple and inexpensive, suitable for a wide range of crops and soil types. It does not require any advanced technology or equipment.

o **Challenges**: Water can be wasted through runoff and evaporation. Inefficient water distribution can lead to waterlogging or soil erosion.

2. **Sprinkler irrigation** :
   o **Technology**: Water is distributed through a system of pipes and sprayed into the air to simulate natural precipitation. Sprinklers can be fixed or mobile.
   o **Advantages**: Efficient use of water with uniform distribution, suitable for hilly terrain. Reduces soil erosion and can be used for a variety of crops.
   o **Challenges**: High initial investment and maintenance costs. Wind can affect water distribution, and water can evaporate before it reaches the ground.

3. **Drip irrigation** :
   o **Technology**: Water is directed directly into the root zone of the plants through pipes and a network of radiators. It is also known as micro-irrigation.
   o **Benefits**: Highly efficient with minimal water waste, drip irrigation saves water and reduces weed growth. It promotes healthy plant growth and higher yields.
   o **Challenges**: High initial installation costs and regular maintenance to avoid clogging the projectors. Not suitable for all types of crops and soils.

4. **Underground irrigation** :
   - ○ **Technique**: Water is applied below the surface of the ground through buried pipes or a network of porous materials.
   - ○ **Benefits**: Reduces evaporation losses and reduces water contact with leaves and stems, reducing the incidence of disease. Provides constant hydration to the root zone.
   - ○ **Challenges**: Expensive to install and maintain. It is difficult to monitor and manage compared to surface irrigation methods.

5. **Rainwater harvesting** :
   - ○ **Technology**: Rainwater collection and storage for agricultural use. Methods include rooftop collection, control booms, and storage tanks.
   - ○ **Benefits**: Provides an additional water source during dry periods, reduces reliance on external water supplies, and promotes groundwater recharge.
   - ○ **Challenges**: Ensuring water quality requires investment in infrastructure and proper maintenance. Limited effectiveness in areas with low rainfall.

6. **Watershed management** :
   - ○ **Techniques**: An integrated approach to water resources management in a watershed, including

soil and water conservation, afforestation, and sustainable land use practices.

- o **Benefits**: Increases water availability, reduces soil erosion, and improves groundwater recharge. Supports sustainable agriculture and rural development.

- o **Challenges**: There is a need to involve the community and coordinate stakeholders. Long-term commitment and follow-up are essential for success.

Influence of irrigation on crop yield and stability

1. **Increased crop yield:**
   - o **Impact**: Efficient irrigation practices ensure a steady supply of water and reduce the risk of crop failures due to drought. This leads to higher and more stable agricultural yields, which contributes to food security.
   - o **Example**: Drip irrigation in Maharashtra vineyards has significantly increased yields and improved fruit quality.

2. **Efficient use of water :**
   - o **Impact: Modern** irrigation methods such as drip and sprinkler systems use water more efficiently, reduce waste, and conserve this precious resource.

This is especially important in areas where water is scarce.

- o **Example**: The introduction of sprinkler irrigation in the agricultural drylands of Karnataka has led to the optimization of water consumption and increased agricultural productivity.

3. **Environmental Sustainability** :
   - o **Impacts: Sustainable** water management practices, such as rainwater harvesting and watershed management, help maintain ecological balance and support the long-term profitability of agriculture.
   - o **Example**: Watershed management projects in Rajasthan have revitalized degraded land, improved water availability, and increased agricultural production.

4. **Challenges and solutions** :
   - o **Challenges**: Implementing efficient irrigation systems can be expensive and requires technical expertise. Farmers could face financial and logistical hurdles when introducing.
   - o **Solution**: Government grants, training programs, and community initiatives can support the widespread adoption of modern irrigation practices. For example, Pradhan Mantri Krishi Sinchai Yojana (PMKSY) provides financial and technical assistance to farmers.

Finally, efficient irrigation methods and water management practices are key to increasing the productivity and sustainability of agriculture in India. By using modern technologies and optimizing water consumption, farmers can improve crop yields, save water, and contribute to sustainable agricultural development.

3.4: Watershed Management

Watershed management is an integrated approach to conserving water and soil resources in a given watershed. This method emphasizes the sustainable management of water resources, the protection of soils, and the promotion of sustainable agricultural practices. Effective watershed management is crucial to increasing water availability, preventing soil erosion, and supporting rural development.

1. **Definition and meaning** :
   - **Watershed**: A watershed is an area of land where all the water that falls into it flows into a common drain, such as a river, lake, or sea. This includes surface water and integrated groundwater.
   - **Relevance**: Watershed management is essential to ensure sustainable use of water resources, prevent soil erosion, improve water quality, and increase agricultural productivity. It also plays an important role in maintaining ecological balance and supporting rural livelihoods.

2. **Components of watershed management** :
   - ○ **Soil and water conservation**: Implementation of measures to prevent soil erosion and increase water storage. Techniques include contour grouping, terraces, retaining dams, and gully plugs.
   - ○ **Afforestation and afforestation**: Planting trees and vegetation to stabilize the soil, improve water infiltration, and increase biodiversity.
   - ○ **Water catchment structures**: Construction of structures such as infiltration basins, agricultural ponds, and control dams for the collection and storage of rainwater for agricultural use and groundwater recharge.
   - ○ **Sustainable land use practices**: Promote crop rotation, agroforestry, and organic farming to maintain soil fertility and reduce environmental impact.
   - ○ **Community Engagement:** Engaging local communities in the planning and implementation of watershed management projects to ensure sustainability and meet local needs.
3. **Watershed Management Process** :
   - ○ **Planning and Evaluation:** Conduct a comprehensive assessment of the watershed to identify issues, resources, and opportunities.

Develop a detailed management plan based on this assessment.

- o **Implementation**: Implementation of the management plan through a series of coordinated activities, such as the construction of water harvesting structures, tree planting, and the implementation of soil protection measures.
- o **Monitoring and Evaluation**: Continuously monitor the progress and impact of watershed management measures. Adjust the plan as needed to achieve the desired result.

4. **Benefits of watershed management** :

- o **Increased water availability**: Better water conservation and enrichment increases the availability of water for agriculture, drinking, and other purposes.
- o **Reduce soil erosion**: Soil protection measures help prevent soil erosion, maintain soil fertility, and reduce sedimentation in water bodies.
- o **Improved agricultural productivity**: Better water management and soil protection practices lead to higher yields and more sustainable farming systems.
- o **Enhanced biodiversity**: Afforestation and reforestation increase biodiversity, provide habitat for wildlife, and enhance ecosystem services.

- Economic and social benefits: Increased water and soil resources support rural livelihoods, improve food security, and contribute to the overall economic development of the region.

5. **Examples of successful watershed management projects in India** :

    - **Sukhomajri Project, Haryana:** This pioneering project focuses on soil and water conservation through community participation. This has led to an increase in water availability, improved agricultural productivity, and better livelihoods for local farmers.

    - **Ralegan Siddhi, Maharashtra**: Led by social activist Anna Hazare, the project transformed a drought-prone village through watershed management practices such as water harvesting, reforestation, and sustainable agriculture. The village has become a model of rural development and self-sufficiency.

    - **Pani Panchayat, Maharashtra**: This initiative promoted equitable water distribution and sustainable water use through community-managed water resources. It has enabled local farmers to take collective action for water conservation and management.

End

Watershed management is a holistic approach to the sustainable management of water and soil resources. By integrating different conservation practices and involving local communities, watershed management projects can significantly increase water availability, prevent soil erosion, and support rural development. These projects not only improve agricultural productivity but also contribute to the overall well-being of rural communities.

3.5: Government measures for the protection of soil and water

The Government of India has implemented various programs and programs to promote soil and water conservation, ensure sustainable agricultural practices, and improve farmers' livelihoods. These initiatives aim to address the challenges of water scarcity, land degradation, and climate change while strengthening the resilience of the agricultural sector.

1. **Pradhan Mantri Krishi Sinchai Yojana (PMKSY):**
   - **Overview**: Launched in 2015, the PMKSY aims to improve agricultural productivity and ensure better use of water resources. It aims to provide a comprehensive and holistic view of irrigation at the district level.
   - **Ingredients**:
     - **Water for Every Farm**: Ensures access to irrigation in all regions through micro-

irrigation and the exploitation of water sources.

- **More Crop Per Drop**: Promotes water-efficient technologies such as drip irrigation and sprinkler irrigation.
- **Integrated Watershed Management (IWMP) Program:** focuses on soil and water conservation, groundwater recharge, and vegetation cover improvement.

  o **Impact**: Increased irrigation efficiency, increased agricultural productivity, and improved water use efficiency.

2. **Soil Health Card Program** :

   o **Overview**: Launched in 2015, the program aims to provide farmers with information on the nutritional status of their soil and recommEndations for the correct fertilizer dosage and soil improvement.

   o **Ingredients**:

   - **Soil Testing**: Regular soil testing to monitor nutrient content and soil health.
   - **Soil Health Map Publishing**: Provide detailed reports on soil health, including nutrient status and corrective actions for farmers.

   o **Impact**: Better soil fertility management, optimized fertilizer use, and higher crop yields.

3. **National Mission for Sustainable Agriculture (NMSA):**
   - o **Overview**: As part of the National Climate Change Action Plan, the NAMS aims to promote sustainable and climate-resilient agricultural practices. It focuses on soil health management, water use efficiency, and conservation agriculture.
   - o **Ingredients**:
     - **Rainfed Area Development (RAD):** Increases the productivity and sustainability of rainfed agriculture through integrated cropping systems.
     - **Soil Health Management (SHM):** Promotes soil testing, organic farming, and increasing soil fertility.
     - **On-Farm Water Management (OFWM):** Improves water use efficiency through micro-irrigation and water-saving technologies.
   - o **Impacts**: Increase resilience to climate change, improve soil health, and sustainable agricultural practices.

4. **Pradhan Mantri Fasal Bima Yojana (PMFBY):**
   - o **Overview**: Launched in 2016, the PMFBY aims to provide farmers with comprehensive crop insurance that covers risks from planting to post-harvest.
   - o **Ingredients**:

- **Opacity**: Protects against natural disasters, pests, and diseases.
    - **Premium subsidy**: Farmers pay a nominal premium, and the state subsidizes the remaining amount.
    - **Use of technology**: Use remote sensing, smartphones, and drones to accurately and quickly assess crop losses.
  - **Impacts**: Reduced financial risks for farmers, increased resilience to climate-related shocks, and greater confidence in agriculture as a livelihood.

5. **Mahatma Gandhi National Rural Employment Guarantee Act (MGNREGA):**
   - **Overview**: Although MGNREGA is primarily an employment program, it plays an important role in soil and water conservation by focusing on the creation of sustainable assets.
   - **Ingredients**:
     - **Water conservation and reclamation**: Construction of dams, agricultural ponds, and rainwater harvesting structures.
     - **Soil protection**: activities such as contouring, terracing, and afforestation.
   - **Impact**: Increased water availability, improved soil health, and increased agricultural productivity.

Future directions and challenges

1. **Improving sustainable practices** :
   - o **Future direction**: Expand the adoption of sustainable agricultural practices such as organic farming, conservation tillage, and integrated farming systems.
   - o **Challenges**: Raising awareness and training farmers, providing them with access to key inputs, and addressing market linkages.
2. **Using technology** :
   - o **Future direction**: Use of advanced technologies such as remote sensing, GIS, and precision agriculture to improve soil and water management.
   - o **Challenges**: High upfront costs, need for technical know-how, and ensuring that the technology reaches smallholder and marginal farmers.
3. **Community involvement** :
   - o **Future direction**: Strengthen public participation in the planning and implementation of soil and water protection projects.
   - o **Challenges**: Ensure effective community engagement, respond to different local needs, and maintain engagement over time.
4. **Political and institutional support** :
   - o **Future direction**: Improve the policy framework and institutional mechanisms to support sustainable land and water management.

- **Challenges**: Coordination across departments, ensuring timely implementation, and monitoring progress.

Finally, the Indian government's soil and water conservation programs have made significant progress in promoting sustainable agriculture. By addressing future challenges and scaling up successful practices, these initiatives can ensure the long-term productivity and resilience of agriculture.

CHAPTER 4: CROP PRODUCTION AND MANAGEMENT

4.1: Crop Classification

Crop production is a fundamental aspect of agriculture, and understanding crop classification is important for effective management and planning. Plants can be classified based on a variety of criteria, including their use, life cycle, and growing season. This classification makes it possible to select crops adapted to the different regions, optimize the use of resources, and guarantee sustainable agricultural practices.

1. **Classification by use** :
   - **Food crops** :
     - **Cereals**: These are the main foods rich in carbohydrates. This is the case, for example, with rice, wheat, maize, barley, and millet.
     - **Legumes**: These are legumes that are rich in protein. Examples include chickpeas, lentils, peas, and beans.
     - **Fruits and vegetables**: These plants provide important vitamins and minerals. Mangoes, apples, tomatoes, and spinach are examples.
   - **Cash crops** :
     - **Oilseeds**: These plants are mainly grown for oil production. Examples include peanuts, sunflower, mustard, and soybeans.

- **Beverage Factories**: These factories are used to manufacture beverages. Examples are tea, coffee, and cocoa.
- **Fiber Plants**: These plants are used to make textiles. Cotton, jute, and linen are examples of this.
  - **Forage crops**: These plants are grown for animal feed. Examples are alfalfa, clover, and feed corn.
  - **Medicinal and aromatic plants**: These plants have medicinal properties or are used for their aroma. Examples include aloe vera, peppermint, and lavEnder.

2. **Life-cycle classification** :
   - **Annual harvests** :
     - These plants complete their life cycle during a growing season. Examples include rice, wheat, and corn.
   - **Biennial crops** :
     - These plants need two growing seasons to complete their life cycle. In the first season, they grow vegetatively and in the second season, they produce flowers and seeds. Carrots, onions, and beets are examples of this.
   - **Perennial crops** :

- These plants live for more than two years and produce flowers and seeds several times in their lifetime. Examples are sugar cane, bananas, and apples.

3. **Classification by growing season** :
   - **Kharif harvests** :
     - These crops are sown at the beginning of the monsoon and harvested in autumn. They need warm, moist weather during their vegetative phase. This is the case, for example, with rice, maize, sorghum, and cotton.
   - **Rabi harvests** :
     - These plants are sown in winter and harvested in spring. They need cool, dry weather for growth and warm weather to mature. Examples include wheat, barley, mustard, and peas.
   - **Zaid Cultures** :
     - These plants are grown during the summer months between the Rabi and Kharif seasons. They need warm weather and are often grown using irrigation. Examples are watermelons, cucumbers, and forage plants.

4. **Classification by botanical families** :

- o **Poaceae (grass family):** This includes grains and forage crops such as rice, wheat, corn, and sugarcane.
- o **Fabaceae (legume family):** This includes legumes and forage crops such as chickpeas, lentils, beans, and clover.
- o **Nightshade (nightshade family):** Includes plants such as tomatoes, potatoes, eggplants, and peppers.
- o **Brassicaceae (mustard family):** This includes crops such as mustard, cabbage, cauliflower, and broccoli.

Importance of crop classification

1. **Value for money** :
   - o **Meaning:** Understanding the classification of plants helps in the optimal use of resources such as water, fertilizers, and pesticides. It allows farmers to effectively plan crop rotations and intercropping systems.
   - o **Example**: Rotating cereals with legumes can improve soil fertility by sequestering nitrogen while growing deep-rooted plants after shallow weeds can increase soil structure.
2. **Pest and disease control** :

- o **Significance**: Crop classification helps control pests and diseases by diversifying crops and disrupting the life cycle of pests and pathogens.
- o **Example**: Alternative crops from different vegetative families can reduce the formation of family-specific pests and diseases.

3. **Market Planning** :
   - o **Significance**: Classifying crops based on their use helps plan the market and meet consumer demand. This allows for efficient allocation of resources and rapid supply of crops to markets.
   - o **For example**, cash crops, which are in high demand, can increase farmers' incomes, while food crops provide food security.

4. **Sustainable agriculture** :
   - o **Relevance**: Crop classification supports sustainable agriculture by promoting biodiversity, improving soil health, and reducing the environmental impact of agricultural practices.
   - o **Example**: Incorporating perennial crops into farming systems can increase biodiversity and provide habitat for beneficial insects.

End

Understanding plant classification is essential for effective crop production and management. It enables farmers to optimize resources, control pests and diseases, plan for market demands, and adopt sustainable farming practices. By classifying crops based on use, life cycle, growing season, and vegetative families, farmers can increase productivity and contribute to a more resilient and sustainable farming system.

4. 2: Crop rotation and polyculture

Crop rotation and mixed cropping are agricultural practices that improve soil health, increase crop yields, and improve farm stability. These practices are essential for effective crop management and play an important role in sustainable agriculture.

1. **Crop rotation** :
   - **Definition**: Crop rotation is the practice of growing different types of crops one after the other on the same parcel of land at different times of the year. This practice helps maintain soil fertility, reduce soil erosion, and control pests and diseases.
   - **Advantages**:
     - **Soil fertility**: Different crops have different nutrient needs and contribute differently to soil health. For example, legumes fix nitrogen in the soil and enrich it for subsequent crops.
     - **Pest and disease management**: Crop rotation interrupts the life cycle of pests and

pathogens and reduces their accumulation in the soil. This practice helps in the natural control of pests and diseases.

- **Improved soil structure**: Rotating deep-rooted plants with shallow roots helps improve soil structure and aeration, promoting better root growth and water infiltration.
- **Weed control**: Crop rotation helps control weeds by changing growing conditions and reducing the spread of weeds.

o **Examples** :

- **Grain-legume rotation**: Alternating between grains (such as wheat or corn) and legumes (such as chickpeas or lentils) improves soil nitrogen levels and overall fertility.
- **Triennial rotation**: A typical three-year crop rotation may include cereals in the first year, legumes in the second, and root crops (such as potatoes or beets) in the third year.

2. **Mixed cropping** :

o **Intercropping**, also known as intercropping, is the practice of growing two or more crops at the same time on the same plot of land. This method maximizes the use of available resources and increases biodiversity.

- o **Advantages**:
  - **Resource optimization**: Companion cultivation optimizes the use of sunlight, water, and nutrients by combining plants with different growth habits and requirements.
  - **Pest and disease management**: Different cropping systems can reduce the spread of pests and diseases, as some plants can repel pests or attract beneficial insects.
  - **Yield stability**: Mixed crops can lead to more stable yields, as the failure of one crop can be compensated for by the success of another.
  - **Better soil health**: Different crops bring different organic residues to the soil, leading to increased organic matter and soil fertility.
- o **Examples** :
  - **Mixed corn and bean crops**: By growing corn and beans together, corn can help beans climb, while legumes fix nitrogen in the soil, which benefits both crops.
  - **Catch crop of millet and groundnuts**: Millet provides shade for groundnuts, and

groundnuts improve soil fertility through nitrogen fixation.

Techniques for efficient crop and intercrop rotation

1. **Planning and selection** :
   - o **Technique**: Carefully select plants that complement each other in terms of nutrient requirements, growth habits, and pest resistance. Plan crop rotations and mixed crop sequences based on local climate and soil conditions.
   - o **Example**: In a rice-wheat system, wheat follows a legume like mung beans to improve the nitrogen content of the soil.

2. **Time and Sync** :
   - o **Technology**: Ensuring that planting and harvesting times for different crops are synchronized to reduce competition for resources and optimize growth.
   - o **Example**: Growing slow-growing and fast-growing plants in mixed cropping to make optimal use of resources without significant competition.

3. **Local Arrangement** :
   - o **Techniques**: Use spatial arrangements such as row catch crops, strip catch crops, and relay catch crops to optimize resource use and improve crop interactions.

- Example: In strip cropping, corn and soybean strips are used alternately to allow for efficient use of sunlight and reduce pest infestations.

4. **Soil and water management** :
   - **Techniques**: Implement soil and water management practices that support crop rotation and mixed cropping, such as mulching, drip irrigation, and biological modification.
   - **Example**: Plant mulch to retain soil moisture and suppress weeds in a mixed tomato and basil growing system.

Successful Implementation Case Studies

1. **Case Study 1: Crop Rotation in Punjab** :
   - **Implementation**: Farmers in Punjab have introduced a rice-wheat-pod rotation system to increase soil fertility and control pests. This crop rotation improved soil health and increased wheat yield.
   - **Results**: This practice led to sustainable soil management, reduced depEndence on chemical fertilizers, and increased crop productivity.

2. **Case Study 2: Mixed Crops in Karnataka:**
   - **Implementation**: In Karnataka, farmers practice mixed cropping by mixing millet and pigeon peas.

This combination optimizes the use of resources and provides mutual benefits.

- o **Results**: This system has led to increased yields, better pest control, and improved soil fertility, which contributes to the sustainability of smallholder farms.

End

Crop rotation and intercropping are an integral part of sustainable agriculture. By understanding and applying these techniques, farmers can improve soil health, naturally control pests and diseases, and achieve stable and improved yields. These practices contribute to the long-term sustainability and resilience of farming systems.

4.3: Integrated Pest Management

Integrated pest management (IPM) is a sustainable approach to pest management that combines different management practices and methods to reduce the use of chemical pesticides and minimize the impact on the environment. Integrated pest management aims to maintain insect populations at acceptable levels while promoting the health of plants and the surrounding ecosystem.

1. **Principles of integrated pest management** :
   - o **Prevention**: The first line of defense is to prevent pests from becoming a threat. These include

breeding resistant plant varieties, crop rotation, and maintaining healthy soils and plants.

- o **Monitoring and identification**: It is important to monitor plants regularly for signs of pests and to identify them correctly. It helps to make informed decisions on the implementation of control measures.

- o **Thresholds:** Set action thresholds, i.e., the level of pest populations at which control measures must be implemented to avoid unacceptable harm or economic loss.

- o **Control methods**: The use of a combination of control methods, including biological, cultural, mechanical, and chemical control methods. Chemical controls are used as a last resort and in the least disruptive way.

2. **Biological control** :

- o **Technique**: Using natural enemies, parasites, or pathogens to control insect populations.

- o **Examples**: introduction of ladybugs to control aphids or use of Trichogramma wasps to control caterpillar pests.

- o **Benefits**: Reduces the need for chemical pesticides, reduces environmental impact, and promotes biodiversity.

3. **Cultural control** :

- o **Techniques**: Change agricultural practices to reduce pest establishment, reproduction, and survival.
- o **Examples**: crop rotation, catch cropping, planting trap crops to avoid extreme pest populations, and adjusting planting dates.
- o **Benefits**: Improves pest management without the use of chemicals, improves soil health, and can increase overall crop productivity.

4. **Mechanical and physical control** :
   - o **Technology**: Using physical methods or mechanical devices to eliminate or eliminate pests.
   - o **Examples** include hand-picking pests, using barriers or screens, using netting, and implementing tillage practices to interrupt the life cycle of pests.
   - o **Benefits**: Provides instant pest control, reduces pesticide use, and is often cost-effective.

5. **Chemical control** :
   - o **Technology**: Application of insecticides to control insect populations, which are used as a last resort in integrated pest management.
   - o **Examples**: Selective use of pesticides, herbicides, and fungicides based on the needs of pests and plants.

- o **Benefits**: Effective in controlling serious pest infestations, protecting crops from significant damage, and ensuring economic viability.

Implementation of integrated pest management

1. **Follow-up and screening** :
   - o **Technique**: Check fields regularly for early signs of insect infestation and determine pest population.
   - o **Examples**: Use of pheromone traps to monitor insect populations or visual inspections to detect signs of disease.
   - o **Benefits**: Early detection allows for early intervention and prevents insect populations from reaching harmful levels.

2. **Decision-making** :
   - o **Technical**: Make informed decisions based on monitoring data, action levels, and economic considerations.
   - o **Example**: Apply biological control when insect populations exceed the limit or timing of pesticide application to coincide with lower stages of pest development.
   - o **Benefits**: Ensures efficient use of resources, reduces unnecessary pesticide applications, and reduces environmental impact.

3. **Education and training** :

- o **Engineering**: Provide training and resources to farmers on IPM principles and practices.
- o **Examples**: Workshop facilitation, distribution of information materials and shows on a farm.
- o **Benefits**: Allows farmers to effectively implement IPM, promote sustainable farming practices, and improve overall farm management.

Case Study on the Successful Implementation of Integrated Pest Management

1. **Case Study 1: IPM in Cotton Production in Maharashtra** :
   - o **Implementation**: Farmers in Maharashtra have adopted integrated pest management practices such as the use of pheromone traps for monitoring, the release of natural enemies, and crop rotation.
   - o **The result**: a significant reduction in pesticide use, improved cotton yields, and improved soil health.
2. **Case Study 2: IPM in Rice Farming in Tamil Nadu** :
   - o **Implementation**: Rice farmers in Tamil Nadu have implemented integrated pest management strategies that include the use of resistant varieties, biological control agents, and regular field monitoring.
   - o **The result**: reduced pest infestation, increased rice productivity, and reduced production costs.

Challenges and future directions

1. **Challenges** :
   - **Introduction**: Farmers may find it difficult to adopt IPM due to a lack of knowledge, resources, or upfront investment.
   - **Knowledge gaps**: Limited access to information and training on IPM practices can hinder effective implementation.
   - **Market pressure**: Demand for aesthetically flawless products can lead to an increase in pesticide use.

2. **Future directions** :
   - **Research and innovation**: investment in research to develop new IPM techniques and tools, including biological control products and pest-resistant plant varieties.
   - **Policy support**: Strengthen strategies and incentives to promote the deployment of integrated pest management and reduce depEndence on chemical pesticides.
   - **Advisory Services**: Enhance agricultural advisory services to provide farmers with timely and accurate information on IPM practices.

End

Integrated pest management is a comprehensive and sustainable approach to pest management in agriculture. By combining biological, cultural, mechanical, and chemical controls, IPM helps reduce pesticide use, protect the environment, and ensure the long-term health of plants and ecosystems. Implementing IPM requires knowledge, planning, and collaboration, but it offers significant benefits for sustainable agriculture.

4.4: Organic farming methods

Organic farming is a method of plant and animal production that involves much more than the disposal of synthetic fertilizers, pesticides, genetically modified organisms, antibiotics, and growth hormones. The goal of this approach is to produce food while maintaining an ecological balance to prevent soil fertility or pest problems. Organic farming combines traditional best practices with modern science to create a sustainable and integrated approach to farming.

Principles of organic farming

1. **Health**: Organic agriculture must maintain and improve the health of the soil, plants, animals, humans, and the planet as a unit and indivisibility.
2. **Ecology**: Organic farming should be based on, work with, simulate, and help maintain living ecological systems and cycles.

3. **Fairness**: Organic farming must be based on relationships that ensure equity in terms of the overall environment and life chances.

4. **Care**: Organic farming must be managed carefully and responsibly to protect the health and well-being of current and future generations as well as the environment.

Important Organic Farming Practices

Soil management: Organic farmers maintain soil health by increasing the natural fertility of the soil. Techniques include crop rotation, green manure, compost, and biological pest control.

- **Crop rotation**: This practice involves growing different crops one after the other on the same land to improve soil health and reduce pest and disease cycles. It helps preserve soil nutrients and reduces soil erosion.

- **Green manure**: Green manure is the process of growing cover crops that are tilled into the soil to add organic matter and nutrients. It improves soil structure, increases nitrogen content, and increases water retention.

- **Compost**: Organic farming relies heavily on composting organic matter that provides important nutrients to the soil. Compost improves soil structure, aeration, and water retention.

- **Biological pest control**: This method uses natural enemies, parasites, and pathogens to control pests and diseases. It helps maintain ecological balance and reduces the need for chemical pesticides.

Use of organic inputs: Organic farming prohibits the use of synthetic inputs. Instead, it relies on organic inputs such as manure, manure, green manure, and biofertilizers to maintain soil fertility and plant health.

- **Compost**: Animal manure is an important source of nutrients for organic farming. It adds organic matter to the soil, improves soil structure, and increases microbial activity.
- **Biofertilizers**: These are living microorganisms that increase the availability of nutrients to plants. Examples are Rhizobium, Azotobacter, and blue-green algae, which bind to atmospheric nitrogen and improve soil fertility.
- **Plant-based pesticides**: Plant extracts such as neem oil, garlic extract, and chili pepper extracts are used to control pests and diseases. They are environmentally friEndly and leave no harmful residues.

Water management: Efficient use of water is important in organic farming. Techniques such as drip irrigation and mulching help to save water and maintain soil moisture.

- **Drip irrigation**: In this method, water is transported directly to the roots of the plants through a network of pipes, reducing water waste and ensuring efficient use.

- **Mulching**: Mulching is the process of covering the soil with organic matter, such as straw, leaves, or compost, to retain moisture, suppress weeds, and improve soil health.

Animal husbandry: Organic farming methods also extEnd to animal husbandry. The animals are fed organic feed, have access to the outdoors, and are not treated with antibiotics or growth hormones.

- **Organic Feed**: Animals are fed organic feed that is free of synthetic additives and genetically modified organisms.
- **Animal welfare**: Organic farming systems give animals a place to move and behave naturally. This improves their health and well-being.

Benefits of Organic Farming

Environmental benefits :

- **Biodiversity**: Organic farming promotes biodiversity through the use of a variety of crops and animal species, which increases the resilience of the ecosystem.
- **Soil health**: By avoiding synthetic chemicals, organic farming maintains soil health, increases organic matter, and increases microbial activity.
- **Water quality**: Reducing the use of synthetic pesticides and fertilizers reduces the risk of water pollution and protects aquatic ecosystems.

- **Climate protection**: Organic farming methods such as carbon sequestration in the soil, reduction of energy consumption, and greenhouse gas emissions contribute to climate protection.

Economic and social benefits :

- **Farmers' income**: Organic products often fetch the highest prices in the market, increasing farmers' incomes.
- **Food security**: Organic farming can contribute to food security by producing safe and nutritious food without relying on synthetic inputs.
- **Community health**: By reducing exposure to harmful chemicals, organic farming promotes better health for farmers and consumers.

The challenges of organic farming

- **Yield level**: Organic farming generally has lower yields than conventional farming, especially during the transition period.
- Labor-intensive: Organic farming requires more labor for practices such as weeding, composting, and pest control.
- **Certification process**: Obtaining organic certification can be time-consuming and expensive for farmers, especially smallholders.
- **Market access**: Organic farmers may struggle to access markets and obtain fair prices for their products.

Case Study on Organic Farming in India

Sikkim: Sikkim is the first fully biological state of India. The government has put in place measures and support systems to promote organic farming, which has led to sustainable farming practices and an increase in biodiversity.

Punjab: Some farmers in Punjab have successfully converted to organic farming and grow crops such as basmati rice, wheat, and vegetables. They saw improved soil health and reduced input costs.

Kerala: Initiatives for organic farming in Kerala have focused on spices such as black pepper, cardamom, and vanilla. These efforts have not only improved soil fertility, but have also increased farmers' incomes through higher prices.

End

Organic farming is a sustainable farming practice that offers many environmental, economic, and social benefits. By adopting organic farming methods, farmers can contribute to a healthier planet and a more resilient agricultural system. Despite the challenges, the growing demand for organic products offers a promising opportunity for the expansion of organic farming in India.

4.5: Use of Technology in Agricultural Production

The integration of technology into agriculture has revolutionized agricultural production, leading to increased efficiency, productivity, and sustainability. Modern technologies enable precision farming practices, reduce resource waste, and provide real-time data for informed decision-making. Here, we explore the different technologies that are changing agricultural production in India.

Precise cultivation

Definition: Precision agriculture involves the use of technology to monitor and manage the variability of growing areas. This approach uses weather, soil, and crop data to optimize agricultural practices.

Components and Benefits :

- **GPS and GIS:** Global Positioning System (GPS) and Geographic Information System (GIS) help map fields and monitor plant health. Farmers can properly use inputs such as fertilizers and pesticides when needed, reducing waste.
- **Remote sensing**: Satellite imagery and drones provide real-time data on plant health, soil conditions, and weather conditions. This information helps farmers make timely decisions about irrigation, pest management, and harvesting.
- **Variable Rate Technology (VRT):** VRT allows for the accurate application of inputs based on field variability. This technology ensures that plants receive the right

amount of nutrients and water, improving yields and reducing costs.

Internet of Things (IoT) in Agriculture

Definition: IoT in agriculture involves the use of interconnected devices and sensors to collect and analyze data on various farming activities.

Application & Benefits :

- **Soil sensors**: IoT-enabled soil sensors measure humidity, temperature, and nutrient content in real time. This data helps farmers optimize irrigation and fertilization programs and ensure healthy plant growth.
- **Climate monitoring**: IoT devices monitor environmental conditions such as temperature, humidity, and precipitation. This information allows farmers to adapt their practices to current weather conditions, reducing the risk of crop failures.
- **Smart irrigation system**: Automated irrigation systems use IoT sensors to transport water exactly when and where it is needed. These systems conserve water and improve crop yields by maintaining optimal soil moisture.

Biotechnology

Definition: Biotechnology involves the use of living organisms and genetic engineering to increase plant production.

Application & Benefits :

- **Genetically modified (GM) crops**: GM crops are modified to have desirable properties such as pest resistance, herbicide tolerance, and better nutrient content. These plants can reduce the need for chemical inputs and increase yields.
- **Tissue culture**: In this technique, plants are grown from cells or tissues in a controlled environment. Tissue culture allows for the rapid propagation of high-yielding, disease-free plants.
- **Marker-Assisted Breeding (SAM):** SAM is a plant breeding method that uses molecular markers to select desirable traits. This technique accelerates the development of improved plant varieties.

Artificial Intelligence (AI) and Machine Learning

Definition: AI and machine learning involve the use of algorithms and data analysis to make predictions and optimize agricultural practices.

Application & Benefits :

- **Predictive analytics**: AI tools analyze historical and real-time data to predict crop yields, pest outbreaks, and weather conditions. Farmers can use this information to plan their activities and mitigate risks.

- **Robotics**: AI-powered robots perform tasks such as planting, weeding, and harvesting with high precision. These robots reduce labor costs and increase the efficiency of agricultural production.

- **Decision Support System (DSS):** AI-powered DSS provides farmers with recommEndations on farming practices based on data analysis. These systems help farmers make informed decisions that increase productivity.

Blockchain technology

Definition: Blockchain technology uses a decentralized digital ledger to record and verify transactions.

Application & Benefits :

- **Traceability**: Blockchain allows agricultural products to be tracked from farm to fork. This traceability ensures food safety and increases consumer confidence in organic and high-quality products.

- **Smart contracts**: Blockchain-based smart contracts automate and enforce agreements between farmers and buyers. These contracts provide transparency and reduce transaction costs.

- **Supply Chain Management**: Blockchain streamlines supply chain processes by providing real-time data on inventory, shipments, and transactions. This technology improves efficiency and reduces losses in the supply chain.

Case Study on the Use of Technology in Indian Agriculture

Case Study 1: Precision Agriculture in Punjab: Farmers in Punjab have adopted precision agriculture techniques using GPS and remote sensing. These technologies have improved the efficiency of water and fertilizer use, resulting in increased crop yields and reduced input costs.

Case Study 2: IoT in Andhra Pradesh: An IoT-based smart irrigation system has been implemented in Andhra Pradesh. These systems monitor soil moisture and weather conditions, optimize water use, and increase crop productivity.

Case Study 3: GM Cotton in Maharashtra: The introduction of GM cotton in Maharashtra has significantly increased cotton yields and reduced the need for chemical pesticides. This biotechnological innovation has improved farmers' incomes and contributed to sustainable agricultural practices.

Case Study 4: AI in Karnataka: An AI-powered predictive analytics tool is being used by farmers in Karnataka to predict weather patterns and pest outbreaks. These tools help farmers plan their activities and minimize crop losses.

End

The introduction of modern techniques in agricultural production is changing Indian agriculture. By using precision agriculture, IoT, biotechnology, AI, and blockchain, farmers can increase productivity, reduce resource waste, and ensure sustainability. These technologies offer promising solutions to the challenges of the agricultural sector and pave the way for a more resilient and efficient agricultural system.

Chapter 5: Gardening and Growing Crops

5.1: Introduction to Gardening

The science and art of horticulture, the cultivation of fruits, vegetables, flowers, and ornamental plants, play an important role in increasing agricultural productivity and diversifying income sources for farmers. Unlike traditional crops, horticultural crops often require more intensive management and care, but they offer higher yields and contribute significantly to nutrition and food security.

Definition and scope:

- **Horticulture:** It includes a wide range of plant breeding activities, including pomology (fruit growing), olive growing (vegetable growing), floriculture (floriculture), and landscaping.
- **Scope:** Goes beyond just crop production to include post-harvest management, value creation, and marketing. This includes the cultivation of plantation crops such as tea, coffee, rubber, and spices.

Importance of gardening:

- **Food security:** Horticultural crops are rich in vitamins, minerals, and antioxidants that contribute to a balanced and nutritious diet. They play an important role in the fight against malnutrition and food security.

- **Economic benefits:** Horticulture offers a higher income per acreage than conventional crops. It offers opportunities for value creation through processing, packaging, and export, thereby increasing farmers' incomes.

- **Job creation:** This sector creates employment opportunities in rural and urban areas, from manufacturing and processing to marketing and retailing.

- **Environmental sustainability:** Horticulture promotes biodiversity, improves soil health through diverse cropping systems, and supports sustainable agricultural practices.

Important subdivisions of horticulture:

1. **Pomology (arboriculture):**
   - **Scope of application:** It includes the cultivation of various fruits such as apples, mangoes, bananas, grapes, and citrus fruits.
   - **Relevance:** Fruit cultivation is essential for the supply of vitamins and minerals and has a high commercial value in both domestic and international markets.

2. **Olive growing (vegetable farming):**
   - **Scope:** Includes the production of vegetables such as tomatoes, potatoes, onions, carrots, and leafy greens.

- **Meaning:** Vegetables are important for fiber, vitamins, and minerals. They have short growth cycles that allow for multiple harvests per year.

3. **Floriculture (floriculture):**
   - **Scope of application:** This includes the cultivation of flowers and ornamental plants for gardens, landscaping, and the floral industry.
   - **Meaning:** Flowers are important for aesthetic, cultural, and ceremonial purposes. The floriculture industry also supports nursery and landscape architecture.

4. **Landscaping and ornamental horticulture:**
   - **Scope:** Includes the design and maintenance of landscapes, gardens, parks, and green spaces.
   - **Meaning:** Improves the urban and rural environment, promotes mental well-being, and supports tourism and recreational activities.

Gardening methods and techniques:

- **Propagation methods:** These include seed multiplication, vegetative propagation (cuttings, grafting, layering), and tissue culture. Each method has its advantages and is chosen according to the plant and the desired characteristics.
- **Plant management:** It includes practices such as pruning, training, pest and disease management, irrigation, and

fertilization to meet the specific needs of horticultural crops.

- **Post-harvest management:** Focuses on reducing post-harvest losses through proper handling, storage, processing, and transportation to ensure quality and extEnd shelf life.

Challenges in horticulture:

- **Climate sensitivity:** Horticultural crops are often more sensitive to climate fluctuations and extreme weather events that require precise management.
- **Pest and disease management:** Intensive agricultural practices can lead to a higher incidence of pests and diseases, requiring integrated pest management strategies.
- **Market access:** Inadequate infrastructure and supply chain issues can make it difficult for farmers to access markets and get fair prices for their products.

Government Initiatives and Support:

- **Programs and Programs:** Various government programs such as the National Horticultural Mission (NHM) and the Mission for the Integrated Development of Horticulture (MIDH) aim to support horticultural development through grants, training, and infrastructure development.
- **Research and development**: Focus on the development of high-yielding, disease-resistant varieties, and sustainable

agricultural practices through agricultural research institutes.

Case Study: Horticulture in Maharashtra:

- **Example:** Maharashtra is a leading state in horticulture, known for its extensive cultivation of grapes, pomegranates, and oranges. The favorable climate of the state, coupled with government support and innovative agricultural practices, has led to a significant increase in horticultural production and exports.

End: Horticulture is a dynamic and important part of agriculture and contributes to economic growth, food security, and environmental sustainability. By adopting improved horticultural practices and taking advantage of government support, farmers can increase their productivity and profitability, ensuring a prosperous future for the region.

5.2: Most Important Fruits and Vegetables

Fruits and vegetables are an essential part of horticulture, provide essential nutrients, and play an important role in agriculture. India, with its different climatic conditions, supports the cultivation of a variety of fruits and vegetables, each with a unique nutritional profile and economic value.

Main crops:

1. **Mango (Mangifera indica):**
   - **Region:** Mainly grown in Uttar Pradesh, Andhra Pradesh, Maharashtra, Karnataka, and Bihar.
   - **Varieties:** Popular varieties include Alphonso, Dasheri, Saffron, Langda, and Banganapalli.
   - **Meaning:** Mangoes, known as the "king of fruits," are rich in vitamins A and C, as well as fiber. They are often eaten fresh, juiced, and used in various culinary dishes.

2. **Banana (Moses species)**
   - **Region:** Tamil Nadu, Maharashtra, Gujarat, Andhra Pradesh, and Karnataka are the major producing states.
   - **Varieties:** The important varieties are CavEndish, Robusta, NEndran, and Rasthali.
   - **Meaning:** Bananas are an important staple food rich in potassium, vitamin C, and vitamin B6. They are eaten fresh, used for cooking, and processed into products such as chips and purees.

3. **Apple (Malus domestica):**
   - **Region:** Mainly grown in Jammu and Kashmir, Himachal Pradesh, and Uttarakhand.
   - **Strains:** Popular varieties include Red Delicious, Golden Delicious, and Royal Gala.

- **Meaning:** Apples are rich in fiber, vitamins C and K, and antioxidants. They are eaten fresh, juiced, and used for baking and cooking.

4. **Grape varieties (Vitis vinifera):**
   - **Region:** Maharashtra, Karnataka, Andhra Pradesh, and Tamil Nadu are the major producing states.
   - **Strains:** The main strains include Thompson Seedless, Anab-e-Shahi, and Bangalore Blue.
   - **Meaning:** Grapes are rich in vitamins C and K as well as antioxidants. They are eaten fresh, dried as raisins, and used in winemaking and juice making.

5. **Pomegranate (Punica granatum):**
   - **Region:** Mainly grown in Maharashtra, Karnataka, Gujarat, and Andhra Pradesh.
   - **Varieties:** The important varieties are saffron, Ganesha and Arakata.
   - **Meaning:** Pomegranates are rich in antioxidants, vitamins C and K, and fiber. They are fresh, pressed, and used in culinary recipes and traditional medicine.

Main vegetables:

1. **Tomato (Solanum lycopersicum):**
   - **Region:** The major producing states are Uttar Pradesh, Karnataka, Andhra Pradesh, Maharashtra, and Tamil Nadu.

- o **Strains:** Popular strains include Pusa Ruby, Arka Vikas, and Roma.
- o **Meaning:** Tomatoes are rich in vitamins A and C, potassium, and lycopene. They are often used for cooking, made into sauces, and eaten fresh.

2. **Potato (Solanum tuberosum):**
   - o **Region:** Uttar Pradesh, West Bengal, Bihar, Gujarat, and Madhya Pradesh are the major producing states.
   - o **Varieties:** The most important varieties are Kufri Jyoti, Kufri Pukhraj, and Kufri Bahar.
   - o **Meaning:** Potatoes are vegetables rich in carbohydrates, vitamin C, and potassium. They are boiled, baked, fried, and used in a variety of dishes.

3. **Onion (Allium cepa):**
   - o **Region:** Maharashtra, Karnataka, Gujarat, Madhya Pradesh, and Bihar are the major producing states.
   - o **Varieties:** The important varieties are Pusa Red, N-53, and Agrifound Light Red.
   - o **Meaning:** Onions are rich in vitamins C and B6 as well as antioxidants. They are often used in cooking, in salads, and as a condiment.

4. **Carrot (Doucus carota):**
   - o **Region:** Uttar Pradesh, Punjab, Karnataka, and Andhra Pradesh are the major producing states.

- o **Varieties:** Popular varieties include Nantes, Pusa Safran, and Early Nantes.
- o **Meaning:** Carrots are rich in beta-carotene, fiber, vitamins K1 and B6, and antioxidants. They are eaten raw, cooked, and used in salads and juices.

5. **Cabbage (Brassica oleracea var. capital):**
   - o **Region:** Uttar Pradesh, Odisha, Bihar, Maharashtra, and Karnataka are the major producing states.
   - o **Varieties:** The main varieties include Pusa Drumhead, Golden Acre, and Copenhagen Market.
   - o **Meaning:** Cabbage is rich in vitamins C and K, fiber, and antioxidants. It is eaten raw in salads, cooked, and used in fermented products like sauerkraut.

Importance of fruits and vegetables:

- **Nutritional benefits:** Fruits and vegetables are essential to a balanced diet and provide vitamins, minerals, fiber, and antioxidants. They help prevent various diseases and promote overall health.
- **Economic impact:** Growing and marketing fruits and vegetables provides farmers with a significant income and contributes to the economy through domestic sales and exports.

- **Employment opportunities:** Horticulture creates many jobs in production, processing, packaging, transportation, and retail, and supports rural and urban livelihoods.
- **Environmental benefits:** Various horticultural practices increase biodiversity, improve soil health, and support sustainable agricultural practices.

Challenges in horticulture:

- **Pest and Disease Management:** Fruits and vegetables are susceptible to a variety of pests and diseases that require effective integrated pest management strategies.
- **Post-harvest losses:** The deterioration of horticultural products leads to significant post-harvest losses and requires efficient handling, storage, and transport infrastructure.
- **Market access:** Farmers often struggle to access the market and get fair prices for their products due to inadequate infrastructure and market connections.
- **Climate change:** Adverse weather conditions and climate change affect the productivity and quality of horticultural crops, requiring adaptable practices and resilient varieties.

Government Initiatives:

- **Programs and Programs:** Government initiatives such as the Mission for Integrated Horticultural Development (MIDH) and Rashtriya Krishi Vikas Yojana (RKVY) support horticultural development through grants, training, and infrastructure development.

- **Research and development**: Focus on the development of high-yielding, disease-resistant varieties, and sustainable agricultural practices through agricultural research institutes.

End: Growing important fruits and vegetables is important for food security, economic growth, and sustainable agriculture in India. By adopting advanced horticultural practices and leveraging government support, farmers can increase productivity, reduce post-harvest losses, and achieve higher profitability.

5.3: Flowers and Landscaping

Floriculture, flower, and ornamental plant cultivation, as well as landscaping, landscaping, and garden and green space maintenance, are essential parts of gardening. These practices enhance aesthetic appeal, contribute to environmental sustainability, and provide economic opportunities through the florist and landscaping industries.

Floriculture:

- **Definition:** Floriculture includes the cultivation of flowers and ornamentals for gardens, landscaping, and the floral industry. This is the production of cut flowers, potted plants, and flowers intEnded for use as ornamental foliage.

- **Scope:** Covers a wide range of activities, from greenhouse production and field cultivation to post-harvest handling and marketing. Flower cultivation also involves the development of new plant varieties and hybrids through breeding programs.

Main flowers in floriculture:

1. **Pink (pink species)**
   - **Region:** Widely used in Karnataka, Maharashtra, Tamil Nadu, and West Bengal.
   - **Varieties:** These include hybrid tea, floribunda, grandiflores, and miniature roses.
   - **Usage:** Primarily used as cut flowers in bouquets and arrangements, as well as for planting gardens and landscaping.

2. **Chrysanthemum (Chrysanthemum spp.)**
   - **Region:** Mainly grown in Karnataka, Maharashtra, Tamil Nadu, and West Bengal.
   - **Varieties:** These include pompoms, sprays, and single flowers.
   - **Usage:** Popular for cut flowers, potted plants, and decorative displays in gardens and landscapes.

3. **Marigolds (Taget species)**
   - **Region:** The major producing states are Uttar Pradesh, Tamil Nadu, Karnataka, and West Bengal.

- o **Varieties:** These include African marigolds (Taget erecta) and French marigolds (Taget patula).
- o **Usage:** Widely used for garlands, decoration, and landscape planting. Marigolds are also appreciated for their insect-repellent properties.

4. **Carnations (Dianthus caryophilus):**
   - o **Region:** Widely cultivated in Himachal Pradesh, Karnataka, and Maharashtra.
   - o **Varieties:** Standard cloves and spray included.
   - o **Use:** Bouquets and their long vases are popular as cut flowers for arrangements because of the diversity of life and colors.

5. **Gerbera (Gerbera gemstone):**
   - o **Region:** Grown in Karnataka, Maharashtra, and Tamil Nadu.
   - o **Varieties:** Offers a wide range of colors and shapes.
   - o **Usage:** Widely used as cut flowers in flower arrangements and as potted plants for indoor and outdoor decoration.

Floriculture practices:

- **Propagation methods:** These include seed propagation, cuttings, division, and tissue culture. Each method has its advantages, depEnding on the type of plant and the desired characteristics.

- **Greenhouse production:** controlled organic farming that allows flowers to be grown all year round. Greenhouses provide optimal growing conditions and protect plants from weather and pests.
- **Post-harvest handling:** This includes proper harvesting, storage, and transportation techniques to ensure the quality and longevity of cut flowers and potted plants.

Landscaping:

- **Definition:** Landscaping includes the design, installation, and maintenance of gardens, parks, and other green spaces. It incorporates plants, aquatic properties, landscaping, and other elements to create an aesthetically pleasing and functional outdoor environment.
- **Scope:** Includes residential, commercial, and public landscaping projects. Landscaping increases property value, provides recreational space, and supports environmental sustainability.

Landscaping Components:

1. **Landscaping:**
   - **Element:** This is the selection and arrangement of plants such as trees, shrubs, flowers, and grasses. Landscaping focuses on plant health, aesthetics, and ecological balance.

- o **Technique:** Plant selection based on climate, soil type, and design preferences. Practices include mulching, pruning, and pest control.

2. **Landscaping:**
   - o **Elements:** This includes the use of non-plant materials such as stones, pavers, fences, water features, and garden structures. Adds structure and functionality to the landscaping landscape.
   - o **Technology:** Design and installation of paths, decks, retaining walls, and decorative elements. The focus is on durability, maintenance, and aesthetics.

3. **Water games:**
   - o **Features:** Includes ponds, fountains, waterfalls, and irrigation systems. The water features give the landscape calm and biodiversity.
   - o **Engineering:** Design and installation of water features to ensure good circulation, filtration, and aesthetic integration into the overall landscaping.

Benefits of Flower and Landscaping:

- **Economic Opportunities:** Flowers and landscaping provide significant economic benefits through the production and sale of flowers, ornamentals, and landscaping services.
- **Environmental sustainability:** These practices promote biodiversity, improve air quality, and support soil and water

conservation. Green spaces also reduce urban heat, and the island effect and improve the ecological balance.

- **Aesthetic and Recreational Value:** Well-designed landscapes and beautiful flowers enhance the aesthetic appeal of homes, public spaces, and commercial properties. They provide a space for recreation and improve mental well-being.

Flower and landscaping challenges:

- **Climate sensitivity:** Flowers and ornamentals are often sensitive to climate fluctuations and extreme weather events that require careful management.
- **Pest and disease control:** High-quality plants in floriculture are susceptible to pests and diseases, requiring integrated pest management (IPM) strategies.
- **Market access:** Farmers and landscapers may face challenges in accessing markets and fair prices for their products due to inadequate infrastructure and market connections.

Government Initiatives:

- **Programs and Programs:** Government initiatives such as the National Horticultural Mission (NHM) and the Mission for the Integrated Development of Horticulture (MIDH) support flowering and landscaping through grants, training, and infrastructure development.

- **Research and development**: Focus on the development of high-yielding, disease-resistant varieties, and sustainable agricultural practices through agricultural research institutes.

Bottom Line: Flowers and landscaping are important components of horticulture and contribute to economic growth, environmental sustainability, and aesthetic improvement. By adopting improved agricultural practices and leveraging government support, farmers and landscapers can achieve increased productivity and profitability and ensure a vibrant future for these regions.

5.4: Cultivation of crops (tea, coffee, rubber, etc.)

Plantation crops, which are usually grown on large estates and require intensive cultivation, are an important segment of horticulture in India. These crops such as tea, coffee, rubber, and various spices are economically and culturally important, contribute to India's export earnings, and provide livelihoods for millions of people.

Tea (Camellia sinensis):

- **Region:** Mainly grown in Assam, West Bengal (Darjeeling), Tamil Nadu (Nilgiris) and Kerala.
- **Varieties:** The main varieties include Assam tea, Darjeeling tea, and Nilgiri tea.

- **Cultivation:** Requires tropical and subtropical climates with high humidity, well-drained clay soil, and elevations between 600 and 2000 m.

- **Processing:** It includes grinding, wilting, rolling, fermentation (for black tea), drying, and sorting. Green tea, oolong tea, and Bemployslack tea differ in their processing methods.

- **Economic importance:** Tea is one of India's largest exports. The tea industry provides work for millions of people, especially in rural and hilly areas.

- **Challenges:** Topics include climate change, pest and disease management, labor shortages, and market fluctuations.

Coffee (types of coffee)

- **Region:** Mainly grown in Karnataka, Kerala, and Tamil Nadu.

- **Varieties:** Arabica (Coffea arabica) and Robusta (Coffea canephora) are the two main varieties grown.

- **Cultivation:** prefers tropical climate with a temperature range of 15-28°C, high humidity, well-drained clay soil, and an altitude of 600-2000m.

- **Processing:** This includes harvesting, pulping, fermentation, drying, peeling, polishing, sorting, and roasting. The processing method affects the taste and quality of the coffee.

- **Economic importance:** Coffee is an important export product that contributes significantly to foreign exchange earnings. The industry supports many small and large producers.
- **Challenges:** Challenges include price volatility, climate change, pest and disease control, and the need for sustainable agricultural practices.

Rubber (Hewe brasiliensis):

- **Region:** Mainly grown in Kerala, Tamil Nadu, Karnataka, and the northeastern states.
- **Cultivation:** It requires a hot and humid climate with temperatures between 25 and 35 °C and well-drained and fertile soil. Rubber trees are usually grown in large plantations.
- **Processing:** The latex is glued to the trees, frozen, and made into plates or blocks.
- **Economic importance:** Rubber is important for the production of tires, industrial products, and medical supplies. The industry supports a large number of smallholder farmers and provides raw materials to various industries.
- **Challenges:** Topics covered include global price volatility, competition from synthetic rubber, and the impact of climate change on yield and quality.

Spices:

1. **Black pepper (Piper nigrum):**
   - **Region:** Mainly grown in Kerala, Karnataka and Tamil Nadu.
   - **Cultivation:** Requires a warm, humid climate with well-drained soil. Often grown as an intermediate crop with coffee and coconut.
   - **Processing**: includes harvesting, drying, and grinding. Black, white, and green peppers are treated differently.
   - **Economic importance:** Black pepper is considered the "king of spices" and is an important export product.
   - **Challenges:** Pest and disease management, climate change, and price volatility.

2. **Cardamom (Cardamom):**
   - **Region:** Mainly grown in Kerala, Karnataka and Tamil Nadu.
   - **Cultivation:** Prefers cool, moist climates with well-drained, semi-shaded clay soil.
   - **Processing**: includes harvesting, drying, and sorting. Cardamom is used as a spice and in traditional medicine.
   - **Economic importance:** Cardamom is known as the "queen of spices" and is highly valued in international markets.

o **Challenges:** high production costs, pest and disease control, and market price fluctuations.

3. **Turmeric (Curcuma longa):**
   o **Region:** Grown in Andhra Pradesh, Tamil Nadu, Karnataka, Odisha, and West Bengal.
   o **Cultivation:** Requires a warm, humid climate with well-drained soil. Typically grown as an annual crop.
   o **Processing:** Includes harvesting, baking, drying, and powder grinding.
   o **Economic importance:** widely used as a spice, in traditional medicine and as a natural dye.
   o **Challenges:** Price fluctuations, climate sensitivity, and quality control.

Economic and social impacts of plantation crops:

- **Job creation:** Plantation crops employ millions of people, especially in rural and hilly areas, and provide livelihoods for smallholder farmers and plantation workers.
- **Export earnings:** These crops are a major contributor to India's export earnings and contribute to the country's foreign exchange reserves.
- **Cultural significance:** Plantation cultures such as tea, coffee, and spices are deeply rooted in India's cultural and culinary traditions.

- **Challenges:** Climate change, market volatility, pest and disease management, and the need for sustainable agricultural practices.

Government Initiatives:

- **Programs and Programs:** Government initiatives such as the Rubber Board, Spices Board, Coffee Board, and Tea Board support the development of plantation crops through research, training, grants, and infrastructure development.
- **Research and development**: Focus on the development of high-yielding, disease-resistant varieties, and sustainable agricultural practices through agricultural research institutes.

End: Plantation crops are important to India's economy, culture, and agricultural landscape. By adopting advanced agricultural techniques, leveraging government support, and addressing challenges such as climate change and market volatility, the plantation sector can achieve sustainable development and contribute significantly to the livelihoods of millions of people.

5.5: Post-harvest management and marketing

Effective post-harvest management and marketing strategies are important for maximizing the value of horticultural crops and plantations. Proper handling, storage, and processing can significantly reduce post-harvest losses, ensure quality, and increase profitability for farmers. In addition, strong marketing systems help farmers reach markets, get fair prices, and meet consumer demand.

Post-harvest management:

1. **Cut:**
   - **Timing:** It is important to harvest at the right stage of maturity to ensure the best quality and shelf life. For example, fruits such as bananas and mangoes are often harvested when they are green and later ripe.
   - **Techniques:** Proper techniques such as hand harvesting, use of tools, and mechanized harvesting minimize damage to produce. For example, using scissors to harvest grapes will help prevent injury and spoilage.

2. **Handling and transport:**
   - **Handling:** Gentle handling of produce during harvesting, packaging, and transportation reduces mechanical injuries. For example, packing apples in padded boxes help prevent injury.
   - **Transportation:** Using refrigerated trucks and maintaining adequate moisture levels during transportation is essential for perishable crops such as flowers and leafy greens.

3. **Cleaning and sorting:**

- o **Cleaning: The** removal of dirt, debris, and agricultural heat through washing and cooling processes helps maintain product quality. For example, if you rinse leafy vegetables with cold water immediately after harvest, the freshness will remain.
- o **Sorting and sorting:** Sorting by size, color, and quality ensures consistency and meets market standards. Sorting tomatoes by size and maturity allows for efficient marketing and pricing.

4. **To save:**
- o **Cold storage:** Cold storage helps maintain low temperatures and extEnd the shelf life of perishable products by controlling humidity. For example, storing apples at 0-4°C significantly increases their shelf life.
- o **Controlled Atmosphere Storage: Advanced** storage techniques such as controlled atmosphere storage regulate oxygen and carbon dioxide levels to slow respiration and delay maturation. It is commonly used for apples and pears.

5. **Resource:**
- o **Primary processing:** This includes activities such as peeling, cutting, juicing, and drying. For example, processing mangoes into pulp or slices increases value and extEnds shelf life.

- Secondary processing: This involves processing the raw product into value-added products such as jams, sauces, cucumbers, and beverages. Processing tomatoes into ketchup and sauces increases their market value.

Sale:

1. **Market:**
   - **Local market:** Farmers can sell their produce at local markets, reducing transportation costs and ensuring freshness. Farmers' markets and local markets are common examples.
   - **Wholesale market:** Selling products on wholesale markets helps reach a wider audience, although it may involve intermediaries. For example, the APMC (Agricultural Produce Market Committee) markets in India facilitate the wholesale of agricultural products.
   - **Export Market:** High-quality products that meet international standards can be exported, resulting in high prices. India exports mangoes, grapes, and spices to various countries.

2. **Value added:**
   - **Packaging:** Attractive and sustainable packaging increases the marketing of products. For example, packaging strawberries in clear, ventilated

containers attracts consumers and preserves freshness.

- o **Branding:** Creating a brand identity helps build trust and loyalty among consumers. For example, "Himalayan apples" or "Alphonso mangoes" are recognized for their quality and origin.

3. **Marketing channels:**
   - o **Direct marketing:** Farmers sell their products directly to consumers through farm kiosks, pick-your-own farms, and online platforms. This eliminates middlemen and increases profits.
   - o **Retail chain:** Supplying products to retail chains and supermarkets ensures a stable market and high prices. For example, the delivery of organic vegetables to stores such as Big Bazaar or Reliance Fresh.
   - o **E-commerce: Online** platforms and applications facilitate direct-to-consumer sales and expand the market reach. Platforms such as BigBasket and Amazon Fresh offer freshly produced deliveries.

4. **State and cooperative support:**
   - o **Marketing Cooperatives: Co-operatives** help farmers market their products together, negotiate better prices, and access resources. For example, the Amul cooperative supports dairy farmers in India.

- o **Government programs:** Various government programs provide financial assistance, training, and infrastructure support for post-harvest management and marketing. The National Horticultural Council (NHB) and the Agricultural and Processed Food Products Export Development Authority (APEDA) provide this support.

Case Study:

1. **Maharashtra Mango Exports:**
   - o **Initiatives:** Alphonso mango farmers in Maharashtra have been successful in penetrating export markets by adhering to international quality standards and using advanced post-harvest technologies.
   - o **Impact:** This has increased farmers' incomes and recognized Alphonso mangoes as a premium product around the world.

2. **Grape processing in Nashik:**
   - o **Initiatives:** Known as the "Wine Capital of India," Nashik has developed a robust grape processing industry that produces wines that meet international standards.
   - o **Impact:** The wine industry has brought significant economic benefits, including increased employment opportunities and grape prices for local farmers.

3. **Marketing of organic vegetables in Karnataka:**

    o **Initiatives:** Organic vegetable farmers in Karnataka have set up direct sales channels through farmers' markets and online platforms.

    o **Impact:** It has improved profitability, reduced reliance on middlemen, and increased consumer awareness of organic products.

End:

Effective post-harvest management and marketing strategies are essential to maximize the value of horticultural crops and plantations. By using cutting-edge technologies, leveraging government support, and exploring diversified marketing channels, farmers can reduce losses, ensure quality, and increase profitability. These efforts contribute to the overall growth and sustainability of the horticultural sector in India.

Chapter 6: Livestock and Poultry Management

6.1: Importance of livestock in Indian agriculture

Livestock plays an important role in India's agricultural landscape and contributes significantly to the country's economy, food security, and rural livelihoods. Integrating livestock into crop production is a traditional practice in India, which offers many benefits to smallholder farmers and the agricultural sector as a whole.

Economic contribution

Livestock contributes significantly to India's agricultural GDP. The sector provides employment and income to millions of rural households, especially marginal communities and small-scale farming communities. Animal products such as milk, meat, eggs, wool, and leather are important components of agriculture.

Dairy farming is an important activity in the livestock sector. India is the largest producer of milk in the world, and the dairy industry provides a stable source of income for millions of farmers. The dairy sector alone accounts for more than 20% of agricultural GDP. The cooperative models implemented by Amul have revolutionized dairy farming in India, increased productivity, and guaranteed fair prices for farmers.

Poultry farming has grown significantly over the past few decades and has become an important part of the livestock industry. India is one of the leading egg and chicken meat-producing countries. The poultry sector provides the population with affordable sources of protein while creating many job opportunities in both rural and urban areas.

Food security and nutrition

Animal products are important for the food security of the Indian population. Milk, meat, and eggs are rich in essential nutrients, including protein, vitamins, and minerals, which are important for the health and growth of individuals. The availability of these products helps to combat malnutrition, especially in rural areas where access to various food sources may be limited.

Agricultural Sustainability

The integration of livestock into crop production improves agricultural sustainability. The project provides electricity for livestock, especially in areas where mechanization is limited. Animal manure is a valuable organic fertilizer that improves soil fertility and crop yields and promotes sustainable agricultural practices.

Livelihood diversification

For many smallholders, livestock farming is used to diversify livelihoods and manage risks. Livestock can be sold in times of financial hardship and provide a safety net against crop failures and other economic shocks. This diversification helps stabilize incomes and increase the resilience of rural households.

Socio-cultural importance

Livestock farming has an important socio-cultural importance in India. Animals such as cows, buffaloes, goats, and poultry are often part of traditional practices and rituals. They are an integral part of various cultural and religious festivals and highlight the deep connection between livestock and the socio-cultural fabric of rural India.

Challenges and opportunities

Despite its importance, the livestock sector faces many challenges that must be addressed to reach its full potential. These challenges include:

- **Disease management: The** prevalence of diseases such as foot-and-mouth disease, brucellosis, and avian influenza poses a significant threat to livestock health and productivity. Effective disease management and control programs are essential to maintaining healthy livestock populations.

- **Feed and feed:** Ensuring the availability of quality and feed is important for animal productivity. India is facing a shortage of green fodder, which requires the adoption of better forage farming practices and effective forage management.
- **Genetic improvement:** Increasing the genetic potential of native breeds through selective breeding and the introduction of high-yielding breeds can improve productivity. The preservation of indigenous breeds adapted to local conditions is also important for genetic diversity.
- **Market access:** Improving market infrastructure and accessibility can help farmers get better prices for their livestock products. Strengthening supply chains and developing value-added products can increase the profitability of the sector.

Government Initiatives

The Indian government has implemented several initiatives to support the livestock sector, including programs to improve animal health, productivity, and market access. Programs such as the Rashtriya Livestock Mission, the Rashtriya Gokul Mission, and the Rashtriya Dairy Yojana focus on sustainable development and promotion of the livestock sector.

In summary, livestock is an essential part of Indian agriculture and contributes to economic growth, food security, and rural livelihoods. Overcoming challenges and seizing opportunities within the sector can increase the productivity, sustainability, and prosperity of millions of farmers across the country.

6.2: Dairy farming

Dairy farming is the cornerstone of the livestock sector in India and plays an important role in rural development, food security, and the national economy. The Indian dairy industry has undergone significant changes in recent years, driven by technological advancements, policy initiatives, and cooperation models.

Historical perspective

The history of dairy farming in India dates back to ancient times, with milk and dairy products being an integral part of the Indian diet and culture. Traditional dairy practices were largely disorganized, and smallholder farmers had few dairy animals. The establishment of the National Dairy Development Board (NDDB) in 1965 marked a turning point in the region and led to the implementation of Operation Flood, the largest dairy development program in the world. This initiative transformed India from a milk-poor country to the world's largest milk producer.

Co-operative model

The cooperative model has played an important role in the success of dairy farming in India. Amul, the largest dairy cooperative, is a great example of how effective this model is. Cooperatives have empowered farmers by providing them with access to markets, fair prices, veterinary services, and inputs such as animal feed. The cooperative structure ensures that profits are distributed fairly among members, improving their livelihoods.

Breed and milk production

India is home to a variety of dairy breeds, including native breeds such as Gir, Sahiwal, and Red Sindhi, as well as hybrids and exotic breeds such as Holstein Friesian and Jersey. Each breed has unique characteristics in terms of milk production, fat content, and adaptation to local conditions.

- **Native breeds:** These breeds are adapted to the local climate and are resistant to disease. They typically produce milk with a high-fat content, which is preferable to conventional dairy products.
- **Hybrids and exotic breeds:** These breeds were introduced to increase milk production. They typically produce larger amounts of milk but need better management and care.

Dairy farming practices

Effective dairy farming practices are essential to optimize milk production and ensure the health and welfare of dairy animals. Key practices include:

- **Diet and nutrition: A** balanced diet is important for milk production and animal health. Farmers use a combination of green forage, dry fodder, and concentrate feed to meet the nutritional needs of dairy animals.
- **Housing and management:** Proper housing protects animals from extreme weather and disease. Clean and well-ventilated homes are essential for maintaining hygiene and reducing stress.
- **Milking methods:** Clean milking practices are important to avoid contamination and ensure milk quality. A regular milking schedule and proper handling techniques help maintain abdominal health.
- **Healthcare:** Regular veterinary checkups, vaccinations, and deworming are essential to keep dairy animals healthy. Disease prevention and management play an important role in maintaining productivity.

The challenges of dairy farming

Despite its successes, dairy farming in India continues to face several challenges that need to be addressed to maintain growth and productivity.

- **Lack of food and feed:** The availability of high-quality food and feed is a major challenge. The lack of green fodder affects milk production and animal health.

- **Health and disease management:** Controlling diseases such as mastitis, foot-and-mouth disease, and brucellosis is important to maintain the health and productivity of the herd.

- **Genetic improvement: It** is necessary to increase the genetic potential of dairy animals through selective breeding and the use of advanced breeding techniques to increase milk production.

- **Market access and infrastructure:** Improved market access and infrastructure for milk collection, storage, and transportation can help farmers get better prices and reduce post-harvest losses.

- **Climate change: The** effects of climate change, such as heat stress and changes in feed availability, are critical to sustaining dairy farming.

Government Initiatives

The Indian government has launched several initiatives to support the dairy sector. Key programs include:

- **Rashtriya Gokul Mission:** Focuses on genetic improvement and the development and conservation of indigenous breeds through the establishment of Gokul Grams (Livestock Care Centers).

- **National Milk Plan:** It aims to increase milk production, improve breed quality, and strengthen the dairy value chain.
- **Pradhan Mantri Matsya Sampada Yojana (PMMSY):** Although the program focuses mainly on fisheries, it also includes provisions for the development of dairy infrastructure and market access.

Prospects

With continued investment in infrastructure, technology, and capacity building, the future of dairy farming in India looks bright. The introduction of modern dairy practices, genetic improvement programs, and improved market access can significantly increase productivity and profitability. Moreover, the growing demand for dairy products at home and abroad is providing new opportunities for Indian dairy farmers.

In end, dairy farming is an important part of Indian agriculture and contributes to economic growth, food security, and rural development. Overcoming challenges and seizing opportunities within the sector can lead to continued growth and prosperity for millions of dairy farmers across the country.

6.3: Poultry

Poultry farming in India has become a dynamic and growing sector that contributes significantly to the agricultural economy. It provides a reliable source of income for smallholders and smallholder farmers while ensuring the supply of affordable protein to the population. This sector includes both the production of broilers for meat and the production of laying hens for eggs.

Historical evolution

The development of poultry farming in India dates back to the early 20th century but gained considerable momentum in the post-indepEndence period. Initially, traditional backyard poultry farming dominated, with native breeds providing eggs and meat for local consumption. The introduction of high-yielding breeds and modern farming practices in the 1960s revolutionized the region and led to the establishment of commercial poultry farms.

Types of poultry farming

- **Broiler farming:** Broilers are chickens raised specifically for meat production. Broiler farming has been growing rapidly due to the increasing demand for poultry meat due to its affordability and nutritional benefits.
- **Laying hen farming:** Laying hens are chickens raised primarily for egg production. Laying hen farming provides farmers with a steady source of income and contributes to food security by providing eggs, protein, and a rich source of essential nutrients.

Breeds and genetics

India has a rich diversity of native poultry breeds such as Asil, Kadaknath, and Vanraja, which are known to adapt to local conditions and be resistant to disease. However, commercial poultry farming mainly uses high-yielding breeds such as White Leghorn for egg production and Cornish Cross for broiler production. These breeds have been bred for high productivity, rapid growth, and efficient feed conversion.

Poultry practices

Effective poultry farming requires careful management of a variety of factors to ensure the health and productivity of birds. Key practices include:

- **Husbandry and environment:** Proper housing is essential to protect poultry from extreme weather, predators, and disease. Modern poultry farms use climate-controlled environments to maintain optimal temperature, humidity, and ventilation.
- **Feed and nutrition:** A balanced diet is important for poultry growth and productivity. Commercial feed formulations are designed to meet the specific nutritional needs of broilers and laying hens, ensuring that they receive the right mix of protein, vitamins, minerals, and energy.
- **Health management:** Health care is important for preventing disease and maintaining the health of the herd.

Regular vaccinations, biosecurity measures, and hygiene practices help prevent the spread of infectious diseases.

- **Breeding and hatching:** Selective breeding programs focus on increasing desirable traits such as growth rate, egg production, and disease resistance. Hatcheries play an important role in supplying poultry farms with high-quality chicks.

The challenges of poultry farming

Despite its rapid growth, the poultry sector in India faces several challenges that need to be addressed to support its growth:

- **Outbreaks:** Poultry farming is susceptible to a variety of diseases, including avian influenza, Newcastle disease, and infectious bursitis. Effective disease control and control strategies are essential to prevent epidemics and losses.
- **Feed costs and availability:** The cost and availability of quality feed is a major concern for poultry farmers. Feed accounts for a significant share of production costs, and fluctuations in feed prices can affect profitability.
- **Market access and infrastructure:** Improving infrastructure and market accessibility is crucial to ensure fair prices for poultry products. Efficient supply chains, cold storage, and processing units are needed to reduce post-harvest losses and improve access to markets.

- **Environmental impact:** Poultry farming generates waste that must be managed effectively to avoid pollution. Sustainable waste management practices such as composting and biogas production can reduce these impacts.

Government Initiatives

The Indian government has implemented various programs to support and promote poultry farming, including:

- **National Livestock Mission:** The objective of this mission is to increase the production and productivity of livestock, including poultry, through improved animal husbandry, feed and feed development, and health care.
- **Poultry Venture Capital Fund:** This program provides financial assistance to farmers and entrepreneurs for the creation and expansion of poultry farms, hatcheries, and processing units.
- **Rural Backyard Poultry Development:** This initiative aims to promote poultry farming in rural areas to improve food security and provide additional income for rural households.

Prospects

With the increasing demand for poultry products at home and abroad, the future of poultry farming in India looks bright.

Technological advances, genetic improvement programs, and improved management practices can further increase productivity and profitability. The sector also has significant potential for value creation through processed poultry products, which can open up new markets and growth opportunities.

In summary, poultry farming is an important part of India's agricultural economy, providing jobs, income, and food security. Addressing challenges and seizing opportunities in the region can lead to sustainable growth and development that benefits millions of farmers and consumers across the country.

6.4: Livestock Disease Management

Effective disease management is important to maintain the health and productivity of farm animals. Diseases can cause significant economic losses, reduce productivity, and even pose risks to human health. It is therefore necessary to implement comprehensive disease prevention and control strategies for sustainable livestock farming.

Common animal diseases

In India, livestock are affected by several diseases, each with different effects on different animal species. Here are some of the most common diseases:

- **Foot-and-mouth disease:** This highly contagious viral disease affects cattle, sheep, goats and pigs. It causes fever, blisters on the mouth and feet, and lameness. Reduced milk production and growth rate can lead to serious economic losses in foot-and-mouth disease.
- **Brucellosis:** This bacterial infection affects cattle, sheep, goats, and pigs. It causes reproductive disorders, including miscarriages, stillbirths, and infertility. Brucellosis is also a zoonosis, which means that it can be transmitted to humans.
- **Mastitis:** This inflammatory udder disease affects dairy cows and reduces milk production and quality. It is caused by a bacterial infection and can be acute or chronic.
- **Newcastle disease:** This viral disease affects poultry and causes shortness of breath, nerve signals, and high mortality. Newcastle disease can wreak havoc on poultry flocks if not managed properly.
- **Small ruminant pest (PPR):** PPR, also known as sheep and goat fever, is a highly contagious viral disease that affects small ruminants. It causes fever, mouth sores, diarrhea, and pneumonia, leading to a high mortality rate.
- **Avian influenza:** Also known as bird flu, this viral infection affects poultry and can cause severe respiratory symptoms and high mortality. Some strains of bird flu can infect humans.

Disease prevention and control strategies

Livestock disease prevention and control requires a combination of management practices, vaccinations, biosecurity measures, and regular health surveillance.

Vaccination: Vaccination is one of the most effective ways to prevent infectious diseases in livestock. Vaccines stimulate the immune system to develop resistance to certain pathogens, thereby reducing the incidence and severity of disease. A routine immunization schedule for all livestock, including cattle, sheep, goats, and poultry, should be followed.

Biosecurity measures: Implementing biosecurity measures helps prevent the introduction and spread of diseases within and between farms. Key biosecurity practices include:

- Control of the movement of animals, people, and equipment in and out of the farm.
- Quarantine of new or sick animals before introduction into the herd.
- Maintain clean and hygienic living and dining areas.
- Use of protective clothing and equipment when handling animals.
- Proper disposal of deadstock and waste.

Regular health surveillance: Regular health surveillance includes regular check-ups and monitoring for early signs of illness. These include:

- Observation of animals for changes in behavior, appetite, or physical condition.
- Perform regular veterinary examinations and diagnostic tests.
- Maintain detailed health records for each animal.
- Implement immediate treatment and isolate sick animals to prevent the spread of the disease.

Good management practices: Adopting good management practices is essential to maintaining animal health and preventing disease. These practices include:

- A balanced diet and clean water to support immune function.
- Ensure adequate housing and ventilation to reduce stress and prevent respiratory illnesses.
- Implement appropriate husbandry practices to prevent genetic disorders and improve the overall health of the herd.
- Regular deworming and parasite control to prevent infections.

Government and veterinary support

The Government of India, in collaboration with veterinary institutions, has implemented several programs and initiatives to support disease management in livestock. Key initiatives include:

- **National Animal Disease Control Program (PNCCD):** It aims to control and eliminate major animal diseases such as foot-and-mouth disease and brucellosis through vaccination and mass surveillance.
- **Veterinary Infrastructure Development:** Improves veterinary services and facilities across the country to provide timely and effective disease management support.
- **Disease Surveillance and Reporting:** Establishes a robust disease surveillance and reporting system to rapidly implement outbreak surveillance and control measures.

Challenges and future directions

While significant progress has been made in disease management, some challenges remain:

- **Scarcity of resources:** limited access to veterinary services, vaccines, and diagnostic tools in remote and rural areas.
- **Raising awareness among farmers:** the need to raise awareness and train farmers in disease prevention and control practices.
- **Emerging Diseases:** The constant threat of emerging and re-emerging diseases due to factors such as climate change, globalization, and changing agricultural practices.

Addressing these challenges requires continued investment in veterinary infrastructure, research and development of new vaccines and diagnostics, and comprehensive training programs for farmers.

In end, effective disease management is crucial for the health and productivity of livestock in India. By implementing preventive measures, ensuring prompt vaccination and treatment, and maintaining good management practices, farmers can protect their livestock from disease, and contribute to sustainable livestock and economic growth.

6.5: Government Livestock Initiatives

The Indian government has recognized the important role of livestock in the agricultural sector and has implemented several initiatives to improve the productivity, health, and well-being of farmers. These initiatives aim to improve genetic potential, ensure animal health, provide financial support, and develop infrastructure.

Important Government Initiatives

1. National Livestock Mission (NLM): Launched in 2014-15, the National Livestock Mission aims to ensure the quantitative and qualitative improvement of livestock production systems. The mission focuses on sustainable development by addressing issues such as animal feed, animal health, and genetic improvement. The main elements are as follows:

- **Breed Breeding:** To improve the genetic potential of native breeds through selective breeding and artificial insemination.
- **Feed and Forage Development:** Promote the cultivation of forage crops and the efficient use of available resources to ensure adequate animal nutrition.
- **Animal Health:** Provide veterinary services, vaccinations, and disease surveillance to maintain animal health and productivity.

2. Rashtriya Gokul Mission: The Rashtriya Gokul mission focuses on the conservation and development of native cattle breeds. Launched in 2014, the mission aims to increase milk production and productivity by:

- **Gokul Gram:** Establishment of integrated animal care centers for indigenous breeds to provide facilities for genetic improvement, nutrition, and health care.
- **Breed Development Program:** Conduct breeding programs to improve the genetic makeup of native breeds while maintaining their purity.
- **Market Development:** Promote marketing initiatives to increase the demand for and value of products from indigenous breeds.

3. National Milk Plan (PND): Launched in 2012, the National Milk Plan (PND) is a long-term initiative to increase milk production and improve dairy animal productivity. The plan focuses on:

- **Breed Improvement:** Expand the coverage of artificial insemination and use improved genetic material to raise dairy breeds.
- **Infrastructure for dairy production:** Develop infrastructure for the supply, processing, and marketing of milk to ensure that farmers receive fair prices.
- **Training and capacity building:** Training of dairy farmers in best practices in animal husbandry, animal husbandry, and feeding.

Pradhan Mantri Matsya Sampada Yojana (PMMSY): Although the PMMSY focuses mainly on the fisheries sector, it also includes elements of livestock development. The main initiatives of the PMMSY related to livestock are:

- **Infrastructure development:** Construction of livestock processing, cold storage, and transportation facilities to improve access to markets.
- **Financial support:** Provide subsidies and financial support to farmers to adopt modern livestock practices and infrastructure.

5. Livestock Insurance Scheme: To protect farmers from financial losses caused by the death of their livestock, the Indian government has introduced the Livestock Insurance Scheme. These systems provide insurance coverage for various livestock such as cattle, buffalo, sheep, goats, and poultry. Key features include:

- **Premium subsidy:** The government subsidizes insurance premiums to make them affordable for small and small farmers.
- **Comprehensive coverage:** Insurance plans cover risks such as accidental death, illness, and natural disasters.

6. Livestock Infrastructure Development Fund (AHIDF): Launched in 2020, the AHIDF aims to promote investment in livestock infrastructure. The Fund provides financial support to:

- **Milk processing and value creation:** Establishment of milk processing units, cold chain infrastructure, and production of value-added products.
- **Meat processing:** Creation of meat processing units, slaughterhouses, and cold storage facilities to improve the meat supply chain.
- **Animal feed:** Development of equipment for the production and distribution of high-quality animal feed and feed.

Impact and Future Directions

These government initiatives have had a significant impact on the livestock sector, leading to improvements in productivity, animal health, and farmers' incomes. The main achievements are as follows:

- **Increased milk production:** Programs such as the Rashtriya Gokul Mission and the Rashtriya Yojana Dairy have contributed to the steady increase in milk production, making India the largest milk producer in the world.
- **Improved animal health:** Veterinary services, disease control programs, and vaccination campaigns have improved animal health and reduced mortality.
- **Genetic improvement:** Breeding programs and artificial insemination have led to the genetic growth of livestock, which has led to increased productivity and higher-quality products.

Challenges and opportunities

Despite these successes, some challenges remain, including:

- **Scarcity of resources:** Ensuring an adequate supply of animal feed remains a challenge, especially in adverse climatic conditions.
- **Raising awareness among farmers:** Raising awareness among farmers and adopting modern livestock practices is important for sustainable development.
- **Infrastructure development:** Sustainable investments in infrastructure such as cold storage, processing units, and

transport are key to improving market access and reducing post-harvest losses.

To address these challenges and opportunities, the government should continue to focus on:

- **Research and innovation:** Investing in research and development to improve livestock genetics, nutrition, and disease management.
- **Capacity building:** Provide training and advisory services to farmers to improve their knowledge and skills in modern livestock practices.
- **Policy support:** Development and implementation of policies that support sustainable livestock development and ensure the well-being of farmers.

In summary, government initiatives play an important role in the growth and development of the livestock sector in India. By addressing challenges and seizing opportunities, these initiatives can increase productivity, sustainability, and economic prosperity for millions of pastoralists across the country.

Chapter 7: Fisheries and Aquaculture

7.1: Overview of fisheries in India

Fisheries and aquaculture play an important role in India's economy, providing livelihoods for millions of people and contributing to food security. With its vast coastline, extensive river systems, and numerous bodies of water, India has a diverse and rich fishery resource base. The sector includes marine, inland, and aquaculture fisheries, each of which contributes to the country's total fish production.

1. **Historical context and development** :
   - **Traditional fishing**: Fishing has been practiced in India for thousands of years, with coastal communities and rivers depEnding on it as their main source of income. Traditional methods include handlines, nets, nets, and spears.
   - **Modern development**: After indepEndence, the Indian government recognized the potential of the fisheries sector and launched various programs to modernize fisheries technology, improve infrastructure, and promote aquaculture. These efforts have significantly increased fish production and productivity.
2. **Current status and production** :

- **Global situation**: India is the world's second-largest fish producer, contributing more than 7% of global fish production. The country's total fish production is about 14.16 million tons per year.

- **Marine Fisheries**: The marine fishing sector includes fishing in the Exclusive Economic Zone (EEZ), which extEnds up to 200 nautical miles from the coast. The main species caught are sardines, mackerel, shrimp, and tuna.

- **Inland Fisheries**: Inland fisheries include fishing in rivers, lakes, reservoirs, and ponds. The most important species are carp, catfish, and freshwater shrimp.

- **Aquaculture**: Aquaculture or fishing is growing rapidly in India. It involves raising fish in controlled environments such as ponds, tanks, and cages. The most important species are carp, tilapia, shrimp, and catfish.

3. **Economic and social impact** :
   - **Employment**: The fisheries sector provides direct and indirect employment to more than 14 million people, particularly in rural and coastal areas. It supports the livelihoods of fishers, fish farmers, processors, and traders.

   - **Income generation**: Fishing contributes significantly to the income of fishers and fish farmers. The development of this sector has increased economic opportunities and improved the living standards of fishing communities.

- o **Food safety**: Fish is an important source of high-quality protein, essential fatty acids, vitamins, and minerals. Per capita fish consumption in India is increasing, contributing to better food security.

4. **Types of fishing** :
   - o **Sea fishing** :
     - **Inshore fishing**: Working in coastal waters and involving small-scale fishers with traditional boats and equipment.
     - **Deep-sea fishing**: Involving larger vessels and more advanced fishing technology to control species found farther from shore.
   - o **Inland fishing** :
     - **River Fishing**: Fishing in rivers and streams.
     - **Reservoir fishing**: Fishing in artificial reservoirs and lakes.
     - **Pond fishing**: Small pond fish farms.
   - o **Aquaculture** :
     - **Freshwater aquaculture**: Farming fish in freshwater environments such as ponds and reservoirs.

- **Brackish water aquaculture**: This includes fish farming in coastal estuaries and lagoons.
- **Aquaculture**: Marine aquaculture, in which marine species are grown at sea or in coastal areas.

5. **Challenges and opportunities** :
   - **Challenges** :
     - **Overfishing**: Overfishing of fish stocks in some areas leads to a decline in fish stocks.
     - **Pollution**: Water pollution from industrial, agricultural, and domestic sources affects fish habitat and health.
     - **Climate change**: The impact of climate change on fish farming, migration, and overall ecosystem health.
     - **Infrastructure**: Inadequate infrastructure for processing, storing, and transporting fish, resulting in post-harvest losses.
     - **Regulatory issues**: The need for effective enforcement to prevent illegal fishing and ensure sustainable practices.
   - **Opportunities** :
     - **Sustainable   Practices**:   Adopting sustainable fishing practices and responsible

aquaculture to ensure long-term productivity and environmental health.

- **Technological advancement**: Using modern technologies in fish farming, processing, and distribution to increase efficiency and reduce losses.

- **State support**: various government programs and initiatives to promote the development of fisheries and aquaculture.

- **Market expansion**: Increased demand for fish and fish products in domestic and international markets, providing growth opportunities.

6. **Government Initiatives and Support** :

   o **Pradhan Mantri Matsya Sampada Yojana (PMMSY):** A flagship program for the sustainable development of the fisheries sector, the improvement of fish production, productivity, and infrastructure.

   o **Blue Revolution**: Initiatives to increase fish production through sustainable practices, capacity building, and technology adoption.

   o **Fish Producer Organizations:** Support for the formation of fish producer organizations to increase collective bargaining power and market access for fish farmers.

- o **Subsidies and financial support**: Provision of subsidies and financial support for the construction of fish ponds, the purchase of equipment, and the establishment of processing units.
- o **Training and advisory services**: Programmes to educate fishers and fish farmers on best practices, sustainable methods, and new technologies.

7. **Technological innovations** :
   - o **Biofloc Technology**: An innovative fish farming method that increases productivity and reduces environmental impact by using waste as feed.
   - o **Recyclability of aquaculture systems (SAR)**: closed-loop systems that recycle water, reduce water consumption, and improve biosecurity.
   - o **Satellite monitoring**: The use of satellite technology to monitor fish stocks, the marine environment, and illegal fishing.
   - o **Genetic improvement**: Research to develop high-yielding, disease-resistant fish breeds to increase aquaculture productivity.

In end, the fisheries and aquaculture sector in India has immense potential to contribute to economic growth, employment, and food security. With the continued support of government initiatives, technological advancements, and sustainable practices, the sector can achieve significant growth and development, ensuring a prosperous future for fishing communities and the nation as a whole.

7.2: Types of Fisheries (Inland and Marine)

Fishing in India can be divided into two types: inland and sea fishing. Each type has different characteristics, practices, and contributions to the fisheries sector as a whole. Understanding these differences is important for effective management and sustainable development.

1. **Inland fisheries**: Inland fisheries include fishing activities in freshwater such as rivers, lakes, reservoirs, ponds, and wetlands. The sector plays an important role in rural livelihoods, food security, and job creation.
   - **River fishing** :
     - **Description**: Fishing activities in rivers and streams. Common fish species include Indian carp (Rohu, Catla, Mrigal), catfish, and freshwater shrimp.
     - **Challenges**: Overfishing, pollution, habitat degradation and diversion of water for irrigation and industrial purposes impact fish populations and biodiversity.
     - **Opportunities**: Implementing sustainable fishing practices, habitat restoration, and

community-based management can increase productivity and biodiversity conservation.

- ○ **Fishing in detention** :
    - ▪ **Description**: Fishing in artificial reservoirs created by the construction of dams on rivers. These waters are an important source of fish production.
    - ▪ **Species**: Mainly Indian head carp, tilapia, catfish and carp.
    - ▪ **Management**: Stock expansion, scientific management, and sustainable fishing practices are essential to maximize the potential of reservoir fisheries.
- ○ **Pond fishing** :
    - ▪ **Description**: Small-scale aquaculture activities conducted in ponds and tanks. Intensive pond management is carried out to maximize fish production.
    - ▪ **Species**: Indian carp, exotic carp, catfish, and tilapia.
    - ▪ **Practical**: Intensive feeding, water quality management, and disease control are important for high productivity.
- ○ **Wetland fisheries** :
    - ▪ **Description**: Fishing in natural wetlands, including floodplains, swamps, and swamps.

These ecosystems are home to a variety of fish and other aquatic organisms.

- **Nature conservation**: Protecting wetlands and adopting sustainable fishing practices can increase fish production and biodiversity conservation.

2. **Sea fishing**: Sea fishing includes fishing at sea and in coastal waters. India has a huge exclusive economic zone (EEZ) of 2.02 million square kilometers, which offers immense potential for marine fisheries.

   o **Inshore fishing** :
     - **Description**: Fishing in coastal waters, usually up to 12 nautical miles from shore. This includes small-scale fishers who use traditional fishing boats and gear.
     - **Species**: Sardines, mackerel, shrimp, anchovies, and crabs are commonly fished.
     - **Challenges**: Overfishing, habitat destruction, pollution, and the effects of climate change pose significant threats to coastal fisheries.

   o **Deep-sea fishing** :
     - **Description**: Fishing is carried out outside the adjacent waters up to the edge of the EEZ. These include larger vessels and more advanced fishing technology.

- **Species**: tuna, swordfish, fried fish, pomfret, and deep-sea shrimp.
- **Management**: Effective management of fish stocks, sustainable fishing practices and international cooperation are essential for the long-term viability of deep-sea fisheries.

o **Deep-sea fishing** :
  - **Description**: Fishing in deep waters, usually beyond the continental shelf. These are vessels and equipment specialized in the fight against deep-sea species.
  - **Species**: deep-sea shrimp, lobster, snapper, and grouper.
  - **Exploration**: Deep-sea fisheries offer opportunities for resource exploration and development, but they require careful management to avoid overfishing and ecosystem loss.

o **Artisanal fishing** :
  - **Description**: Small, traditional fishing activities organized by coastal communities. These fisheries are characterized by low investment, simple equipment, and limited accessibility.
  - **Significance:** Small-scale fisheries provide livelihoods for millions of coastal dwellers

and play an important role in food security and cultural heritage.

- **Support**: Strengthening support for small-scale fishers through capacity building, infrastructure development, and market access can improve their sustainability and economic well-being.

3. **Aquaculture**: Aquaculture, or fish farming, complements inland and marine fisheries by providing an additional source of fish production. It is the breeding, breeding, and harvesting of fish in controlled environments.

    o **Freshwater aquaculture** :

        - **Description**: Fish farming in freshwater environments such as ponds, reservoirs, and reservoirs.

        - **Species**: Indian carp, tilapia, catfish, and freshwater shrimp.

        - **Practical**: intensive management including feed, water quality control, and disease management to maximize production.

    o **Brackish water aquaculture** :

        - **Description**: Fish farming in saltwater environments such as estuaries, coastal lagoons, and tributaries.

        - **Species**: shrimps, mud crabs, sea bass, and canon.

- **Benefits**: High economic returns and employment opportunities, especially in coastal areas.
- o **Aquaculture** :
  - **Description**: Marine aquaculture in which marine animals are raised at sea or in coastal areas.
  - **Species**: selfish (groupers, snappers), shellfish (oysters, mussels), and seaweed.
  - **Benefits**: Uses coastal and offshore areas for fish production, reduces pressure on wild fish stocks, and contributes to food security.

4. **Sustainable action and management** :
   - o **Regulations and policies**: Effectively implement rules and policies to manage fish stocks, prevent overfishing, and protect aquatic ecosystems.
   - o **Community-based management**: Involving local communities in the management and conservation of fisheries resources to ensure sustainable practices and equitable benefits.
   - o **Technological innovation**: Introducing modern technologies in aquaculture, fishing gear, and processing to increase efficiency, reduce environmental impact, and improve product quality.
   - o **Research and Development**: Ongoing research on fish farming, health management, and sustainable

practices to support the growth and development of the fisheries sector.

After all, inland and marine fisheries and aquaculture are an integral part of India's fisheries sector. It is important to understand the unique characteristics and challenges of each type of fishery to develop effective management strategies and ensure the sustainable development of the land. With the continued support of government initiatives, technological advancements, and community engagement, India's fisheries and aquaculture can make significant progress and contribute to the country's food security and economic growth.

7.3: Aquaculture Practices

Aquaculture, or fish farming, is the controlled cultivation of aquatic organisms such as fish, crustaceans, mollusks, and aquatic plants. It is a growing sector in India that contributes significantly to the country's fish production, food security, and rural development. DepEnding on the water body, the type, and the type of farming system, different aquaculture practices are used.

1. **Freshwater aquaculture** :
   o **Pond culture** :
     - **Description**: The most common method of freshwater aquaculture, in which fish are raised in mud or concrete ponds.

- **Species**: Indian carp (Rohu, Catla, Mrigal), exotic carp (carp, grass carp), catfish and tilapia.
- **Practice**: Regular feeding, water quality management, stocking density control and disease surveillance are essential to maintaining healthy fish stocks.
- **Advantages**: high production efficiency and ability to control environmental conditions.

- **Tank culture :**
  - **Description**: Fish farming in concrete, plastic, or metal recessed tanks.
  - **Species**: catfish, tilapia, and ornamental fish.
  - **Benefits**: better water quality control and easy monitoring of fish health and growth.
  - **Challenges**: High initial investment and the need for ongoing water quality management.

- **Cage culture :**
  - **Description**: Fish are raised in suspEnded cages in water bodies such as lakes, reservoirs, and rivers.
  - **Species**: Exotic species such as Indian carp, catfish, and tilapia.
  - **Advantages**: Utilizes existing water bodies without excavation and allows for higher stocking densities.

- **The idea**: Good water quality management and protection against poachers and poaching are needed.

2. **Brackish water aquaculture** :
   - **Shrimp farming** :
     - **Description**: Shrimp farming in saltwater ponds typically found in coastal areas.
     - **Species**: Black tiger shrimp (Penaeus monodon) and white leg shrimp (Litopenaeus vannamei).
     - **Practice**: Pond preparation, stocking with disease-free re-larvae, regular feeding, water quality monitoring, and disease management.
     - **Economic impact**: Higher economic returns due to the demand for shrimp exports.
     - **Challenges**: epidemics, water salinity management, and environmental impacts.
   - **Crab culture** :
     - **Description**: Rearing crabs in saltwater ponds or pens.
     - **Species**: Mud crab (Scylla serrata).
     - **Practice**: Hatchery rearing, pond preparation, feeding with natural and prepared feed, and regular health monitoring.

- **Advantages**: High market price and demand in domestic and international markets.
- **The idea**: requires careful management of water quality and melt cycles.

3. **Aquaculture** :
   - **Marine fish farming** :
     - **Description**: Farming of marine fish in coastal waters or the open ocean.
     - **Species**: Grouper, snapper, sea bass, and pompano.
     - **Practice**: Use of floating or submerged cages, regular feeding, monitoring of environmental conditions, and disease management.
     - **Advantages**: High growth rate and efficient use of coastal and offshore areas.
     - **Challenges**: High initial investments, harsh maritime conditions, and regulatory requirements.
   - **Shellfish farming** :
     - **Description**: Farming of shellfish such as oysters, mussels, and clams in coastal waters.
     - **Convenient**: Use racks, rafts, or longlines to raise shellfish, regularly monitor water quality, and harvest at appropriate sizes.

- **Benefits**: Environmental benefits of water filtration and housing construction, as well as the high market price.
- **The idea**: changes in water quality and sensitivity to the possible effects of pollution and algal blooms.

  o **Seaweed farming** :
- **Description**: Cultivation of algae in coastal areas with ropes, nets, or floating rafts.
- **Species**: Kappaphycus alvarezii, Gracilaria and Sargassum.
- **Practical**: Selection of suitable locations, regular cleaning, and harvesting of algae.
- **Advantages**: Used in food, cosmetics, pharmaceuticals, and biofuels; environmentally friEndly and sustainable.
- **Challenges**: Requires clean, nutrient-rich water and is vulnerable to environmental changes.

4. **Integrated Multi-Trophic Aquaculture (IMTA):**
   o **Description**: An advanced aquaculture system that combines the cultivation of different species from different trophic levels into a single system.
   o **Ingredients**: Usually fish, shellfish, and seaweed.

- **Benefits**: Nutrient recycling improves environmental sustainability by reducing waste and improving the overall health of the ecosystem.
- **Example**: Fish provide nutrients to algae, which in turn support the growth of shellfish by improving water quality.

5. **Sustainable aquaculture practices** :
- **Water Quality Management**: Regularly monitor and maintain water quality parameters such as dissolved oxygen, pH, temperature, and ammonia levels.
- **Feed Management**: The use of balanced, high-quality feeds to ensure optimal growth and reduce waste. Adopt feed conversion efficiency (FCE) practices.
- **Disease prevention**: implementation of biosecurity measures, regular health check-ups, vaccinations, and use of probiotics and immunostimulants.
- **Mitigate environmental** impacts: use organic fertilizers, and adopt environmentally friEndly practices such as waste management and habitat conservation.

6. **Government Initiatives and Support** :
- **Financial support**: Programs such as Pradhan Mantri Matsya Sampada Yojana (PMMSY) provide

financial support for the establishment of aquaculture farms, hatcheries, and processing units.

- o **Training and capacity building**: Training programs and advisory services to educate farmers on best practices, sustainable methods, and technological innovations in aquaculture.

- o **Research and Development**: To help research institutions develop better reproductive technologies, disease management strategies, and sustainable aquaculture practices.

7. **Challenges and opportunities** :

- o **Challenges**: Disease outbreaks, water pollution, high upfront investment costs, climate change impacts, and market access.

- o **Opportunities**: Expansion of domestic and international markets, technological advancements, integrated cropping systems, and diversification into high-quality varieties.

8. **Technological innovations** :

- o **Recyclability of aquaculture systems (SAR):** closed-loop systems that recycle water, reduce water consumption, and improve biosecurity.

- o **Biofloc Technology**: Uses beneficial microbial communities to convert waste into food, improve water quality, and reduce feed costs.

- o **Smart aquaculture**: Using sensors, IoT, and data analytics to monitor and manage aquaculture operations to improve efficiency and productivity.

In summary, aquaculture practices in India are diverse and dynamic, with significant potential to improve fish production, food security, and rural development. By adopting sustainable practices, leveraging technological innovation, and supporting government initiatives, the aquaculture sector can experience significant growth and contribute to the country's economic prosperity and environmental sustainability.

7.4: Sustainable Fisheries Management

Sustainable fisheries management is crucial to ensure the long-term viability of fish populations, the health of aquatic ecosystems, and the livelihoods of fisheries-depEndent communities. This includes implementing practices and policies that balance environmental, economic, and social objectives to maintain fish stocks at sustainable levels.

1. **Principles of sustainable fisheries management** :
   - o **Ecosystem-based management**: Focusing on the whole ecosystem, including the relationship between species and their habitats, rather than focusing on a single species.

- o **Precautionary approach**: take proactive measures to prevent overfishing and habitat destruction, even in the face of scientific uncertainty.
- o **Adaptive management**: Ongoing monitoring and adaptation of management practices based on new science and changing environmental conditions.
- o **Stakeholder participation**: Involve fishers, local communities, scientists, policymakers, and other stakeholders in the decision-making process to ensure diversity of perspectives and shared responsibilities.

2. **Regulatory framework** :
   - o **Fishing quotas and limits**: Setting catch limits and quotas based on scientific assessments of the size and reproductive rates of the fish population to prevent overfishing.
   - o **Fishing seasons and regions**: Implement seasonal closures and protected areas to allow fish populations to multiply and grow to minimize the impact on Endangered species.
   - o **Gear restriction**: Regulate the types of fishing gear used to reduce bycatch, minimize habitat damage, and protect juvenile fish.
   - o **Licenses and** permits: Licenses and permits are required for fishing activities to control the number of anglers and ensure compliance.

3. **Fish stock assessment and monitoring** :
   - o **Population surveys**: Conduct regular surveys and assessments to estimate the size, distribution, and health of fish populations.
   - o **Data collection**: Collecting data on catch rates, fishing effort, and environmental conditions to make management decisions.
   - o **Satellite and remote sensing**: The use of satellite technology and remote sensing to monitor fishing activities, track fish migration, and detect illegal fishing.

4. **Habitat protection and restoration** :
   - o **Marine Protected Areas (MPAs):** Establish MPAs to protect critical habitats such as hatcheries and nurseries from fishing and other human activities.
   - o **Restoration Projects**: Implement habitat restoration projects such as mangrove reforestation and coral reef restoration to improve fish habitat and biodiversity.
   - o **Pollution control**: Reduce pollution from agricultural wastewater, industrial discharges, and plastic waste to improve water quality and protect aquatic ecosystems.

5. **Reduction of bycatch** :
   - o **Selective fishing gear**: Develop and promote the use of selective fishing gear, such as turtle

exclusion devices (TEDs) and bycatch reduction devices (BRDs), to reduce bycatch and protect non-target species.

- ○ **Best Practices**: Train fishers on best practices for handling and releasing bycatch to increase the survival rate of discontinued species.

6. **Adaptation to climate change** :

- ○ **Impact assessment**: Assessing the impacts of climate change on fish populations, habitats, and fishing communities to develop adaptive management strategies.

- ○ **Resilient practices**: Promote resilient fishing practices to reduce vulnerability to climate change, such as diversified fisheries strategies and sustainable aquaculture.

- ○ **Reducing** the carbon footprint: Promoting the adoption of energy-efficient technologies and practices to reduce the carbon footprint of the fishing industry.

7. **Community-Based Fisheries Management (CBM):**

- ○ **Local empowerment**: Empowering local communities to manage their fisheries resources through co-management agreements and participatory governance.

- ○ **Traditional knowledge**: Integrate traditional ecological knowledge with scientific research to develop effective and culturally appropriate management practices.

- o **Capacity building**: Provide training and support to fishing communities to improve their capacity to sustainably manage resources and diversify their livelihoods.

8. **Economic incentives for sustainability** :
- o **Certification and eco-label**: Promote certification schemes such as the Marine Management Council (MSC) and the Aquaculture Management Council (ASC) to promote sustainable fishing practices and create market incentives.

- o **Grants and financial support**: Provide grants and financial support for sustainable fishing practices, habitat restoration, and alternative livelihoods.

- o **Market Access**: Facilitate market access for sustainably caught fish and fishery products to increase economic benefits for fishers.

9. **Government initiatives and international cooperation** :
- o **National policies and programs**: Implementation of national policies and programs to support sustainable fisheries management, such as the National Fisheries Policy and the Pradhan Mantri Matsya Sampada Yojana (PMMSY).

- o **International agreements**: Participate in international agreements and organizations such as the Food and Agriculture Organization of the United Nations (FAO) Code of Conduct for Responsible Fisheries to promote global cooperation and shared responsibility.

- o **Research and Development**: Investing in research and development to improve understanding of fish populations, ecosystems, and sustainable management practices.

10. **Challenges and opportunities** :

- o **Challenges**: Overfishing, habitat destruction, pollution, climate change, and illegal, unreported, and unregulated (IUU) fishing pose significant challenges to the sustainable management of fisheries.

- o **Opportunities**: Technological advances, increased stakeholder engagement, and global collaborations provide opportunities to improve the sustainability of fisheries and ensure the long-term health of aquatic ecosystems.

Finally, sustainable fisheries management is essential to maintain healthy fish populations, protect aquatic ecosystems, and support the livelihoods of fishing communities. By implementing comprehensive management strategies, engaging stakeholders, and promoting sustainable practices, India can achieve a balance between conservation and economic growth, ensuring a prosperous future for its fisheries and aquaculture sector.

7. 5: Government Initiatives and Support in Fisheries and Aquaculture

The Government of India has implemented various initiatives and measures to support the fisheries and aquaculture sector, recognizing their importance for food security, job creation, and economic growth. These initiatives aim to increase productivity, ensure sustainability, and improve the livelihoods of fishing communities.

1. **Pradhan Mantri Matsya Sampada Yojana (PMMSY):**
   - **Objective**: To bring about the Blue Revolution through the sustainable and responsible development of the fisheries sector in India.
   - **Ingredients**:
     - **Infrastructure development**: Construction of fishing ports, fish landing centers, cold storage facilities, and ice factories.
     - **Aquaculture development**: Promote freshwater, brackish, and marine aquaculture through financial support for pond farming, feed, and seeds.
     - **Post-harvest management**: development of value-added products, fish processing units, and marketing infrastructure.
     - **Fisheries Management**: Strengthen fisheries management and management,

including fish stock assessment and conservation measures.

- o **Impact**: The program aims to increase fish production, increase exports, create jobs, and ensure the sustainable use of fisheries resources.

2. **Blue Revolution** :
   - o **Objective**: To increase fish production and productivity through various interventions in aquaculture, capture fisheries, and post-harvest infrastructure.
   - o **Main activities** :
     - **Developing aquaculture**: promoting intensive aquaculture practices, integrated fish farming, and the use of Biofloc technology.
     - **Sustainable practices**: Promote sustainable fishing practices and the conservation of fisheries resources.
     - **Capacity building**: Training and skills development of fishers and fish farmers.
   - o **Results**: Significant increase in fish production, improved fishermen's incomes, and promotion of sustainable fishing practices.

3. **National Fisheries Development Board (NDDB):**

- o **Objective**: To increase fish production and productivity, improve infrastructure, and ensure the well-being of fishers.
- o **Features** :
  - ▪ **Project Funding**: Provide financial support for fisheries and aquaculture projects.
  - ▪ **Technical assistance**: Provide technical advice and support for modern aquaculture practices and fisheries management.
  - ▪ **Research and development**: Supporting research projects aimed at developing new technologies and improving existing practices.
- o **Impact**: Improved infrastructure, increased fish production, and better management of fisheries resources.

4. **Fish Producers' Organizations (FFPOO):**
  - o **Objective**: To organize fish farmers into producer organizations to increase their collective bargaining power and improve market access.
  - o **Advantages**:
    - ▪ **Economies of scale**: Collective purchasing of inputs and mass marketing of products to reduce costs and improve profitability.

- **Capacity building**: Training and capacity-building programs to improve skills and knowledge.
- **Market Linkages**: Establish a direct relationship with buyers and processors to ensure better price realization.
  - o **Results**: Strengthen fish farmers, improve incomes, and improve access to markets.
5. **Regulation and management of marine fisheries:**
   - o **Objective**: To ensure the sustainable exploitation of marine fishery resources and to protect the interests of traditional fishers.
   - o **Rules** :
     - **Fishing Bans**: Seasonal catch limits that allow fish populations to multiply and increase.
     - **Gear restriction**: Regulating the use of certain types of fishing gear to prevent overfishing and protect juveniles.
     - **Marine Protected Areas (MPAs):** Establish MPAs to conserve critical habitat and biodiversity.
   - o **Impact**: Improved sustainability of marine fisheries, protection of fisheries resources, and improved livelihoods of traditional fishers.
6. **Financial support and grant:**

- Programs: Various programs provide financial support and grants for the establishment of aquaculture facilities, the purchase of vessels and fishing gear, and the development of post-harvest infrastructure.
- Advantages:
  - Reduced financial burden: Access to affordable credit and subsidies reduces the financial burden on fishers and fish farmers.
  - Increased productivity: Financial support for modern equipment and practices increases productivity and profitability.
- Results: increased investment in fisheries and aquaculture, improved productivity, and improved livelihoods.

7. Training and consulting services :
   - Objective: To improve the skills and knowledge of fishers and fish farmers through training and advisory services.
   - Activities :
     - Workshops and seminars: Organization of workshops and seminars on best practices, sustainable methods, and new technologies.
     - On-Farm Demonstration: Demonstration of modern aquaculture practices and sustainable fishing practices on farms.

- **Extension Services**: Provide technical advice and support by extension officers and helplines.
  - o **Impact**: Improved knowledge and skills, increased adoption of best practices, and increased productivity.

8. **International cooperation** :
   - o **Agreements and** partnerships: India works with various international organizations and countries to promote sustainable fisheries management and increase trade.
   - o **Advantages**:
     - **Technology transfer**: Access to cutting-edge technologies and best practices from other countries.
     - **Market Access**: Improved international market access for Indian fish and fishery products.
   - o **Results**: improved management practices, increased exports, and strengthened international relations.

9. **Research and development** :
   - o **Institutes**: Research institutes such as the Central Institute of Fisheries Technology (CIFT) and the Central Institute of Freshwater Aquaculture (CIFA) research the development of new technologies and the improvement of existing practices.

- o **Objective** :
  - **Breeding and genetics**: Development of high-yielding, disease-resistant fish breeds.
  - **Disease Management**: Research on ways to prevent and control fish diseases.
  - **Sustainable practices**: Develop sustainable aquaculture practices and improve fisheries management.
- o **Impact**: Increased productivity, reduced disease incidence, and sustainable use of resources.

10. **Challenges and opportunities** :
  - o **Challenges**: Climate change, pollution, overfishing, habitat destruction, and limited access to credit and markets are major challenges for the fisheries sector.
  - o **Opportunities**: Technological advances, increased domestic and international demand for fish, and government support provide opportunities for growth and development in the sector.

In summary, the Indian government has implemented several initiatives to support and develop the fisheries and aquaculture sector. These initiatives aim to increase productivity, ensure sustainability, and improve the livelihoods of fishers and fish farmers. Continued support through technological advancements and sustainable practices will ensure the long-term growth and prosperity of India's fisheries sector.

Chapter 8: Marketing and Trade of Agricultural Products

1: Structure of agricultural markets in India

Agricultural marketing in India plays an important role in ensuring that farmers receive fair prices for their products, that consumers have access to quality products, and that the agricultural sector remains sustainable and profitable. The structure of agricultural markets in India is diverse and includes various stakeholders, institutions and mechanisms that facilitate the transport of agricultural products from farms to consumers.

1. **Agricultural markets at a glance** :
   o **Definition** : Agricultural markets are systems or environments in which the buying and selling of agricultural products takes place. These marketplaces include physical marketplaces, online platforms, and various intermediaries.
   o **Significance**: Efficient agricultural markets allow farmers to sell their produce at lucrative prices, reduce post-harvest losses, and provide consumers with a steady supply of agricultural products.

2. **Types of Agricultural Markets** :
   o **Primary Market (Village Market):**
     ▪ **Description** : These are small markets in rural areas where farmers sell their products

directly to local consumers or small-scale traders.

- **Characteristics** : Limited infrastructure, low volume of business and often informal in nature.
- **Roll** : Serves as the first point of sale for many small and small farmers, providing them with immediate money for their products.

- **Secondary market (Mandi or wholesale market):**
  - **Description** : Large markets are typically located in semi-urban or urban areas, where primary market products are collected and sold to wholesalers, processors and retailers.
  - **Features** : Better infrastructure, higher volume of business, and more formal business practices.
  - **Role**: To act as an important link between primary markets and End consumers, ensuring the distribution of agricultural products over a wide geographical area.

- **Terminal Market** :
  - **Description** : Large centralized markets where production processors from different regions, exporters and wholesalers are used for final sale.

- **Features** : Advanced infrastructure, high trading volume, and sophisticated trading mechanism.
- **Role** : To act as the last point of consolidation before accessing or exporting agricultural processors.

o **Rural periodical market** :

- **Description** : Temporary markets that take place on certain days of the week in rural areas where farmers and traders gather to buy and sell produce.
- **Characteristics** : lack of permanent infrastructure, seasonal and periodic nature and often at a convenient distance from villages.
- **Role** : To enable farmers to sell their surplus produce and consumers to buy new products.

3. **Regulated Markets (APMC):**

o **Agricultural Markets Committees (AMCs):**

- **Description** : Established under state law to regulate the marketing of agricultural products and ensure fair trade practices.
- **Functions**: To facilitate price transparency, prevent exploitation of farmers by

intermediaries and provide the necessary infrastructure for marketing.

- **Infrastructure** : Marketplaces, storage facilities, sorting and sorting units, weighbridges and auction platforms.
- **Challenges** : Issues such as market fragmentation, inadequate infrastructure, variable market fees, and bureaucratic hurdles.

4. **Cooperative marketing** :
   - **Description** : A system in which farmers pool their produce and market it together through cooperatives to ensure greater bargaining power and higher prices.
   - **Examples** : Amul (dairy cooperative), NAFED (National Federation for the Marketing of Agricultural Cooperatives).
   - **Benefits** : Reduced reliance on middlemen, better price realization, access to market information, and better post-harvest management
   - **Challenges** : Management inefficiency, lack of expertise, and limited access to certain areas.

5. **Private Market** :
   - **Description** : Markets operated by private companies, including corporate buyers, contract cultivation agreements, and private mandis.

- o **Role** : Offer alternative marketing channels, increase efficiency, and often offer better value and infrastructure than traditional markets.
- o **Challenges** : Regulatory issues, competition with CMPAs, and potential exploitation if not properly monitored.

6. **Electronic market (e-market):**
   - o **Description** : Digital platforms that facilitate the buying and selling of agricultural products through online auctions and transactions.
   - o **Examples** : e-NAM (National Agriculture Market), Agribazaar and other private electronic markets.
   - o **Benefits** : price transparency, wider market access, reduced transaction costs, and real-time market insights.
   - o **Challenges** : Farmers' digital literacy, internet connection issues, and early resistance to adoption.

7. **Marketing channels** :
   - o **Direct sales** : Farmers sell directly to consumers, processors or retailers without intermediaries. These include farms, farmers' markets, and direct online sales.
   - o **Intermediate sales** : These are intermediaries such as commission agents, wholesalers, and retailers who facilitate the transportation of products from the farmer to the consumer.

- Contract farming : Agreements between farmers and buyers (processors, exporters, or retailers) in which the buyer provides the inputs and agrees to purchase the products at predetermined prices.

8. **Supporting Infrastructure** :
   - **Storage facilities** : Warehouses, cold stores, and warehouses that prevent post-harvest losses and maintain product quality.
   - **Transportation** : Road, rail and air transportation networks that facilitate the transportation of agricultural products from farms to markets.
   - **Market Information System** : Platforms that provide real-time information on prices, demand, supply, and market trEnds to help farmers make informed decisions.

9. **Government Initiatives** :
   - **e-NAM (National Agriculture Market):** An e-commerce platform to integrate APMC markets across the country, allowing farmers to sell their products anywhere in India.
   - **Rural Agricultural Markets (Villages):** Development and modernization of rural haats (markets) into villages to provide better marketing opportunities for farmers.

- o **Prime Minister Kisan Samman Nidhi** : Direct support for farmers' income, improving their financial stability and purchasing power.

10. **Challenges and opportunities** :
- o **Challenges** : Market fragmentation, inadequate infrastructure, price volatility, market inefficiencies, and limited access to credit and market information.
- o **Opportunities** : Digitalization of markets, improved infrastructure, policy reforms, promotion of direct sales and cooperatives, and expansion of market interdepEndencies.

In summary, the structure of agricultural markets in India is complex and multidimensional, involving different types of markets, stakeholders, and mechanisms. Understanding this structure is essential to improve market efficiency, ensure fair prices for farmers, and develop effective strategies to improve the entire agricultural marketing system. By addressing challenges and seizing opportunities, India's agricultural markets can be transformed to better meet the needs of farmers and consumers.

8.2: Marketing Channels and Institutions

Agricultural marketing channels and institutions are important to ensure that agricultural products reach consumers efficiently and that farmers receive fair prices for their products. These channels include various intermediaries, processes, and structures that facilitate the movement of goods from farms to markets. Understanding these channels and institutions helps to find ways to improve the marketing efficiency and sustainability of the agricultural sector.

1. **Marketing channels at a glance** :
   - **Definition** : Marketing channels refer to the channels through which agricultural products pass from producers to consumers. These channels include direct sales, intermediate sales, and institutional markets.
   - **Meaning** : Effective marketing channels reduce transaction costs and post-harvest losses, ensuring that farmers get better prices while consumers have access to fresh and affordable produce.

2. **Types of Marketing Channels** :
   - **Direct Marketing** :
     - **Farmers' markets** : Farmers sell their products directly to consumers at local markets, cutting out the middleman. This channel offers new products to consumers and higher margins to farmers.
     - **Farm sales** : Farmers sell their farm products directly to consumers or retailers who come to the farm. This reduces transportation costs and allows farmers to get a larger share of the retail price.

- **Community Supported Agriculture (CSA):** Consumers subscribe to regular delivery of fresh produce directly from farmers. This model provides initial capital for farmers and ensures a stable market for their products.

o **Intermediate Marketing** :

- **Commissionaires** : Farmers sell their products to commissionaires who act as intermediaries between farmers and wholesalers or retailers. These agents charge commissions for their services.

- **Wholesalers** : Large quantities of products are sold to wholesalers, who then distribute them to retailers or processors. Wholesalers play an important role in collecting products from many farmers and ensure a constant supply.

- **Retailers** : Retailers purchase products from wholesalers or directly from farmers and sell them to End consumers. Retail channels include supermarkets, grocery stores, and street vEndors.

o **Institutional market** :

- **Public procurement** : Government agencies purchase agricultural products at the minimum support price (MSP) to support farmers and maintain buffer stocks. These shares are used for public distribution and food security programs.

- **Contract farming** : Farmers enter into agreements with companies or processors to grow specific crops. Customer will provide resources, technical support, and guaranteed pricing for the Products.

3. **Important Marketing Institutions** :
   - **Agricultural Markets Committees (AMCs):**
     - **Role** : The CMPAs regulate the buying and selling of agricultural products in designated markets. They aim to prevent exploitation by farmers by ensuring transparent prices and fair trade practices.
     - **Functions** : Licensing merchants, auctioning products, collecting market fees, providing infrastructure, and resolving disputes.
     - **Challenges** : market fragmentation, high market fees, bureaucratic inefficiencies and limited market access for smallholder farmers.
   - **Cooperatives** :

- **Role** : Cooperatives allow farmers to pool their resources and market their products collectively, increasing their bargaining power and reducing their depEndence on middlemen.
- **Examples** : dairy cooperatives (e.g. Amul), horticultural cooperatives and multi-purpose agricultural cooperatives.
- **Benefits** : Improved price realization, access to market information, credit facilities, and improved post-harvest management.
- **Challenges** : Management inefficiency, lack of expertise, and limited geographic reach.

- **Private Market** :
  - **Role** : Private companies establish markets that operate outside of the traditional CMPA framework. These markets often offer better infrastructure, higher prices and more efficient services.
  - **Examples** : central purchasing offices for companies, private mandis and chain stores.
  - **Benefits** : Increased competitiveness, better prices for farmers, and market efficiency.
  - **Challenges** : Regulatory barriers, the potential for monopolistic practices, and the need for strict quality standards.

- o **E-marketing platforms** :
  - **Role: Digital** platforms facilitate the online trade of agricultural products, connecting farmers directly with buyers across the country.
  - **Examples** : e-NAM (National Agriculture Market), Agribazaar and Private e-Marketplace.
  - **Benefits** : price transparency, wider market access, reduced transaction costs, and real-time market insights.
  - **Challenges** : Farmers' digital literacy, internet connection issues, and early resistance to adoption.

4. **Government Initiatives and Support** :
   - o **e-NAM (National Agricultural Market):**
     - **Objective** : To create a unified national market by integrating APMC markets across the country via an online trading platform.
     - **Functions** : Online trading, pricing, transparency of transactions and dissemination of market information.
     - **Impact**: Improved market access for farmers, better price realization, and reduced market inefficiencies.
   - o **Rural Agricultural Market (village):**

- **Objective** : To develop and modernize existing rural areas (markets) into well-equipped villages in order to provide better marketing opportunities for farmers.
- **Functions** : Provision of infrastructure, storage facilities and direct market connection for farmers.
- **Impact** : Improved market access, reduced post-harvest losses, and better prices for farmers.

  o **Agricultural Marketing Infrastructure (AMI):**
  - **Objective** : To develop and strengthen the market infrastructure, including storage, processing and transport facilities.
  - **Components** : Construction of warehouses, cold stores, packing stations and sorting units.
  - **Impact** : Increase market efficiency, reduce waste and improve the quality of agricultural products.

5. **Challenges and opportunities** :
   o **Challenges** : Market fragmentation, inadequate infrastructure, price volatility, market inefficiencies, and limited access to credit and market information.
   o **Opportunities** : Digitalization of markets, improved infrastructure, policy reforms, promotion

of direct sales and cooperatives, and expansion of market interdepEndencies.

6. **Role of financial institutions** :

- o **Credit facilities** : Provide loans to farmers for production, marketing, and post-harvest activities through institutions such as NABARD (National Bank for Agriculture and Rural Development) and commercial banks.

- o **Insurance**: Agricultural insurance plans to protect farmers from crop failures due to natural disasters and market fluctuations.

- o **Support Programs** : Government programs provide financial assistance and grants for the development of commercialization infrastructure and capacity building.

8.3: Agricultural Marketing Reforms

Agricultural marketing reforms have played an important role in the transformation of the agricultural sector in India. Historically, the agricultural marketing system in India has been characterized by many middlemen, inefficient supply chains, and a lack of proper infrastructure, which has often resulted in low yields for farmers and high prices for consumers.

The path of agricultural marketing reforms began after indepEndence, with the government aiming to create a more organized and efficient marketing system. The establishment of regulated markets or mandis under the Agricultural Products Market Committee (APMC) Act has been an important step towards this goal. The purpose of these mandis was to provide farmers with a central space to sell their produce, ensure fair prices, and reduce exploitation by middlemen.

Important reforms and measures over the years In recent years, several important reforms have been introduced to increase the efficiency and transparency of agricultural marketing:

1. **CMPA Model Law of 2003:** The law aims to liberalize the agricultural marketing sector by allowing private markets, direct marketing, and contract farming. It was intEnded to reduce the monopoly of CMPAs and promote competition.

2. **National Agricultural Market (e-NAM), 2016:** Launched to integrate existing Mandis into a unified online marketplace platform, e-NAM aims to create a unified national market for agricultural commodities that provides farmers with better prices and access to a wider range of buyers.

3. **The Agriculture Act of 2020: The** Agricultural Trade and Commerce (Promotion and Facilitation) Act, the Agreement on Pricing and Agricultural Services for Farmers (Authorization and Protection), and the Essential Raw Materials (AmEndment) Act were introduced to further liberalize the agricultural market. These laws aimed

to give farmers more freedom to sell their produce outside of APMC mandis, encourage contract farming, and regulate the storage of essential goods.

Impact of these reforms on farmers and agricultural markets
The impact of these reforms has been significant, but not without controversy and challenges:

- **Improved market access:** Reforms such as the e-NAM platform have expanded market access for farmers, allowing them to reach a wider audience and get better prices for their products.
- **Less reliance on middlemen:** By encouraging direct selling and contract farming, farmers can now bypass middlemen, reduce costs, and improve their profit margins.
- **Price increases: The** introduction of online platforms and increased competition have led to better prices that benefit both farmers and consumers.
- **Challenges and resistance:** Despite these achievements, some reforms, including the 2020 Farm Bills, have been met with resistance from farmer groups concerned about the potential dismantling of the APMC system and the risks of exploitation by large corporations.

Case Studies and Examples of Successful Implementation

- **Maharashtra:** The state has been at the forefront of the adoption of the CMPA Model Law, which allows for private procurement and direct sales. This has improved farmers' efficiency and they have received better awards.

- **Karnataka: The** implementation of the e-NAM platform in Karnataka has yielded positive results, with farmers benefiting from transparent pricing and reduced market fees.

- **Punjab and Haryana:** Although these states have robust APMC systems, the introduction of reforms has intensified the debate on the need to modernize and integrate domestic markets.

Finally, agricultural marketing reforms have had a significant impact on the agricultural scenario in India. While there are ongoing challenges and debates, these reforms aim to create a more efficient, transparent, and farmer-friEndly marketing system that ultimately contributes to the growth and sustainability of the agricultural sector.

8.4: Exporting and Importing Agricultural Products

India's agricultural sector plays an important role in the global market, as the country is one of the largest exporters and importers of various agricultural products. Understanding trEnds, key commodities, trade policies, and challenges is essential to maximizing the benefits of the agriculture industry.

Overview of India's Agricultural Exports and Imports India has a diverse portfolio of agricultural exports and imports that reflects the country's vast agricultural landscape. Over the years, agricultural exports have increased significantly, which contributes to the national economy and strengthens India's presence in the global market. At the same time, imports are necessary to meet domestic demand for certain raw materials that are not produced in sufficient quantities or are not grown domestically.

India exports a wide range of agricultural products, including key raw materials:

1. **Rice:** India is the world's largest exporter of rice, with significant exports of both basmati and non-basmati varieties. The main importers are countries in the Middle East, Africa, and Southeast Asia.
2. **Spices:** India is famous for its spice exports, which include black pepper, cardamom, turmeric, and cumin. These spices are in high demand all over the world due to their quality and diverse culinary uses.
3. **Tea and coffee:** India is a major exporter of tea and coffee, with significant exports to countries such as Russia, the United Kingdom, and the United States.
4. **Fruits and vegetables:** Fresh fruits (such as mangoes, bananas, and grapes) and vegetables (such as onions, potatoes, and tomatoes) are the main export products.
5. **Cotton:** India is one of the largest producers and exporters of cotton, with major markets in China, Bangladesh, and Vietnam.

6. **Sugar:** India exports sugar mainly to countries in Asia and Africa, contributing to the global sugar supply.

India imports a range of agricultural products to meet domestic demand, including:

1. **Edible oils:** India is the largest importer of edible oils such as palm oil, soybean oil, and sunflower oil, mainly from Indonesia, Malaysia, and Argentina.
2. **Legumes:** To meet the protein needs of its population, India imports pulses such as lentils, chickpeas, and peas from Canada, Australia, and Myanmar.
3. **Wheat:** India sometimes imports wheat to supplement domestic production, especially during low-yield years.
4. **Fruits:** Some fruits such as apples, kiwis, and almonds are imported to meet the growing demand for diverse and exotic fruits.

Trade policies and agreements that impact agricultural trade shape India's agricultural landscape, including:

1. **Agricultural Export Policy 2018:** The policy aims to double agricultural exports by 2022 through various measures such as infrastructure development, export promotion, and improved market access.
2. **Free Trade Agreements (FTAs):** India has signed several free trade agreements with countries and regional blocs to reduce tariffs and improve trade opportunities. Notable

agreements include the South Asian Free Trade Area (SAFTA) and the India-ASEAN Free Trade Agreement.

3. **Import duties and quotas:** India regulates the import of agricultural products through tariffs and quotas to protect domestic producers and ensure food security. These measures are regularly adapted to domestic supply and demand conditions.

4. **Plant hygiene and sanitation (SPS) measures:** India adheres to international SPS standards to ensure that exported and imported agricultural products meet safety and quality requirements. These measures help to maintain the competitiveness of Indian exports in world markets.

Challenges and Opportunities in Agricultural Trade The agricultural sector in India faces several challenges and opportunities:

Challenges:

1. **Infrastructure:** Inadequate infrastructure, including storage facilities, cold chains, and transportation networks, can lead to post-harvest losses and affect the quality of exports.

2. **Trade barriers:** Tariff and non-tariff barriers imposed by importing countries can restrict market access for Indian agricultural products.

3. **Compliance with standards:** Meeting international standards for quality and safety can be challenging for smallholders and smallholder farmers.

4. **Market volatility: Fluctuations** in global markets and changes in trade policy can affect the sustainability of agricultural trade.

Opportunity:

1. **Diversification:** Expanding the range of export products and entering new markets can increase business opportunities.

2. **Value creation:** Focusing on value-added products such as processed foods and organic products can increase export revenue.

3. **Technological Advancements:** The introduction of modern agricultural practices and technologies can improve productivity and quality and make Indian products more competitive in the global market.

4. **Government support:** Leveraging government initiatives and support programs can help farmers and exporters overcome challenges and seize business opportunities.

In end, India's agricultural export and import sector is vital to the country's economy and food security. By addressing the challenges and seizing the opportunities, India can grow its agricultural business, to the benefit of farmers, consumers and the wider economy.

8.5: Role of e-commerce in the marketing of agricultural products

The integration of e-commerce into agricultural marketing has revolutionized the way farmers sell their products and how consumers buy agricultural products. E-commerce platforms offer several benefits, including wider market access, better price realization, and increased transparency, making them increasingly popular in the agricultural sector.

Introduction to e-commerce in agriculture E-commerce in agriculture refers to the buying and selling of agricultural products and services through online platforms. This digital marketplace allows farmers to reach a wider audience, including consumers, retailers, and institutional buyers, without the constraints of physical markets. The proliferation of smartphones and the internet in rural areas has accelerated the adoption of e-commerce in agriculture.

Benefits of e-commerce for farmers and consumers

1. **Greater market reach:**
   - **Farmers:** E-commerce platforms allow farmers to access a large market beyond their local mandis. They can connect with buyers from different

regions, grow their customer base, and reduce their reliance on local markets.

- o **Consumers:** Consumers enjoy the convenience of purchasing fresh produce directly from the farmer. You'll have access to a diverse range of products, including organic and specialty products that may not be available locally.

2. **Best Achievement of Awards:**

- o **Farmers: By** bypassing middlemen, farmers can sell their products directly to consumers or retailers while ensuring better price realization. This direct correlation helps farmers keep a larger share of the profits.

- o **Consumers:** Competitive pricing on e-commerce platforms often results in lower prices for consumers, as fewer intermediaries reduce the overall cost.

3. **Improved transparency:**

- o **Farmers:** E-commerce platforms provide real-time insights into market prices, demand trEnds, and buyer preferences. This transparency helps farmers make informed decisions about what to grow and when to sell.

- o **Consumers:** Detailed product information, including origin, quality, and certification, allows consumers to make informed purchasing decisions.

Reviews and ratings further increase transparency and trust.

4. **Waste reduction:**
    o **Farmers:** Effective supply chain management and direct sales through e-commerce platforms reduce the time it takes to reach consumers and reduce spoilage and waste.
    o **Consumers:** Access to fresh, high-quality products is improved and the likelihood of purchasing defective products is reduced.

Popular e-commerce platforms and their impact on agricultural marketing

1. **Ninjacart:**
    o **Overview:** Ninjacart connects farmers directly with retailers and businesses, using technology to streamline the supply chain and reduce waste.
    o **Impact:** By cutting out the middleman, Ninjacart ensures that farmers get better prices for their products. The platform also ensures on-time payments, improving the financial stability of farmers.

2. **Agricultural market:**
    o **Overview:** Agribazaar is an online marketplace that facilitates the trading of agricultural products. It

offers services such as auctions, logistics, and financing.

- o **Impact:** The platform supports farmers by providing them with a transparent and efficient way to sell their produce. It also helps farmers access credit and insurance services while reducing their financial risks.

3. **Village:**
   - o **Overview:** Dehat is an agri-tech platform that provides End-to-End solutions to farmers, including access to inputs, advisory services, and market connections.
   - o **Impact:** The integrated rural approach supports farmers along the agricultural value chain and increases productivity and profitability. The market allows farmers to sell their products at competitive prices.

4. **BigHaat:**
   - o **Overview:** BigHaat is an online platform that provides farmers with agricultural inputs such as seeds, fertilizers, and pesticides, as well as market connection services.
   - o **Impact:** By providing high-quality inputs and access to a wider market, BigHaat helps farmers improve their yields and incomes. The platform's

advisory services also help farmers adopt best practices.

Future prospects and potential development of e-commerce in agricultural marketing The future of e-commerce in agricultural marketing looks promising, driven by technological advances, increasing Internet penetration and supportive government policies. Key trEnds and potential areas for growth include:

1. **Blockchain technology:**
   - **Efficiency:** Blockchain can improve the traceability and transparency of the agricultural supply chain and ensure the authenticity and quality of products. This technology can also streamline transactions and reduce fraud.

2. **Artificial Intelligence and Machine Learning:**
   - **Performance:** AI and ML can analyze large data sets to predict market trEnds, optimize pricing, and improve supply chain efficiency. These technologies can help farmers make data-driven decisions and increase productivity and profitability.

3. **Government Initiatives:**
   - **Potential:** Government programs and policies to promote digital agriculture and internet connectivity in rural areas can accelerate the adoption of e-commerce in agriculture. Initiatives such as the

Digital India campaign and the National Agriculture Market (eNAM) aim to create a more integrated and efficient agricultural market.

4. **Integration with financial services:**

   o **Efficiency:** E-commerce platforms can be integrated with financial services to provide farmers with easy access to credit, insurance, and payment solutions. This integration can help farmers better manage their finances and invest in improving their farming practices.

Finally, e-commerce has the potential to transform agricultural marketing by providing farmers with wider access to markets, better price realization, and greater transparency. As technology advances and internet connectivity improves in rural areas, e-commerce will play an increasingly important role in the agricultural sector, driving growth and sustainability.

Chapter 9: Agricultural Finance and Insurance

9.1: Sources of Financing for Agriculture

Agricultural finance is important for the growth and stability of the agricultural sector. It provides farmers with the capital they need to invest in modern equipment, high-quality inputs, and infrastructure to ensure increased productivity and income stability. Understanding the different sources of agricultural finance can help farmers access the funds they need for their farms.

Traditional sources of agricultural finance

1. **LEnder:**
   - **Overview:** Money lEnders have historically been a major source of financing for farmers, especially in rural areas where formal banking services are limited.
   - **Pros:** Quick and easy access to funds with no collateral or bulky paperwork.
   - **Cons:** High interest rates and farming practices often lead to debt traps for farmers.
2. **FriEnds and family:**
   - **Overview:** Farmers often rely on loans or financial support from friEnds and family.

- o **Pros:** Flexible repayment terms and low or no interest rate.
- o **Cons: Limited availability** of funds and potential stress on personal relationships.

Official sources of agricultural finance

1. **Commercial banks:**
   - o **Observation: Commercial** banks provide short-, medium- and long-term loans to farmers for a variety of agricultural activities.
   - o **Types of loans:** farm loan, equipment loan, livestock loan, and farm development loan.
   - o **Benefits:** Structured loan products with reasonable interest rates and repayment terms.
   - o **Cons:** The length of the application process and strict eligibility criteria can be a barrier for small and small farmers.

2. **Credit unions:**
   - o **Overview:** Cooperative banks operate at the village, district, and state levels and provide loans to farmers through cooperatives.
   - o **Types of loans:** Seasonal Agricultural Loans (SAO), equipment and infrastructure term loans, and marketing loans.
   - o **Advantages:** Familiarity with local conditions, member-centric approach, and low interest rates.

- o **Disadvantages:** Limited financial resources and potential management inefficiencies.

3. **Regional Rural Banks (RRBs):**
   - o **Comment:** RRBs are state-owned banks established to serve rural areas and provide loans to the agricultural sector.
   - o **Types of loans:** agricultural loan, dairy production loan, poultry loan, and micro-irrigation and horticulture loan.
   - o **Advantages:** Financial products adapted to rural and agricultural needs, proximity to rural communities.
   - o **Cons:** Limited capital base and depEndence on government support.

4. **Microfinance Institutions (MFIs):**
   - o **Overview:** MFIs provide small loans to rural farmers and entrepreneurs, often through self-help groups (SHGs).
   - o **Types of loans:** Microloans for agricultural inputs, livestock, small appliances, and other rural businesses.
   - o **Pros:** Easy access to credit, minimal paperwork, and flexible repayment plans for small and small farmers.

o **Cons:** Higher interest rates than formal banking institutions and potential challenges in expanding operations.

Government-sponsored programs and programs

1. **Kisan Credit Card System (KCC):**
   o **Overview: The** KCC program, introduced in 1998, provides farmers with timely and adequate credit for their agricultural needs.
   o **Benefits:** Simplified access to credit, flexible procurement options, and coverage for agricultural production and secondary activities.
   o **Eligibility:** Farmers, tenants, oral tenants, and sharecroppers engaged in agriculture and related activities.

2. **Pradhan Mantri Fasal Bima Yojana (PMFBY):**
   o **Overview:** A government-backed crop insurance program that provides financial assistance to farmers in the event of crop failures due to natural disasters, pests, and diseases.
   o **Benefits:** Comprehensive risk protection, low premiums, and support for post-harvest losses.
   o **Eligibility:** Farmers who grow declared crops in the notified areas, including those who have benefited from institutional loans.

3. **Pradhan Mantri Kisan Samman Nidhi (PM-KISAN):**

- o **Overview:** A direct income support program introduced in 2019 that provides financial support to smallholder and smallholder farmers.
- o **Benefits:** Regular income support of Rs 6,000 per year, which is paid directly into farmers' bank accounts in three equal installments.
- o **Eligibility:** All landowning farm families with cropland, except institutional landowners and certain high-income categories.

Non-Bank Financial Companies (NBFCs) and Agritech Platforms

1. **NBFC:**
   - o **Overview:** NBFCs play an important role in lEnding to the agricultural sector, especially in areas underserved by traditional banks.
   - o **Types of loans:** Equipment financing, working capital loans, warehouse receipt financing, and farm business loans.
   - o **Benefits:** Flexible credit products, fast disbursements, and innovative financing solutions.
   - o **Cons:** High interest rates and potential regulatory challenges.
2. **Agritech Platform:**

- o **Overview:** Agritech platforms use technology to provide farmers with access to finance, market connections, and advisory services.
- o **Examples:** Countryside, BigHaat, and Agrostar.
- o **Benefits:** Better access to credit through digital platforms, transparency, and tailor-made financial products for farmers.

Finally, the diverse sources of agricultural finance in India cater to the diverse needs of farmers, from traditional lEnders to modern agritech platforms. By understanding and using these sources effectively, farmers can get the financing they need to improve their farming practices, increase productivity, and achieve financial stability.

9.2: Role of NABARD and other institutions

The National Bank of Agriculture and Rural Development (NABARD) and other financial institutions play an important role in supporting agricultural financing and development in India. These institutions provide the necessary financial resources, implement development programs, and provide technical assistance to increase the productivity and sustainability of the agricultural sector.

National Bank for Agriculture and Rural Development (NABARD)

1. **Observation and installation:**
   - **Foundation:** NABARD was founded in 1982 by a parliamentary act to promote sustainable and equitable agriculture and rural development.
   - **Mission:** To provide and regulate credit and other facilities to promote and develop agriculture, small-scale industry, cottage and village industry, handicrafts, and other rural trades.
2. **Main functions of NABARD:**
   - **Loans:** NABARD offers refinancing to financial institutions that lEnd to agriculture and the rural sector. These include commercial banks, cooperative banks, and regional rural banks (RRBs).
   - **Development Programs:** NABARD designs and implements various development programs to improve rural infrastructure, promote sustainable agricultural practices, and increase farmers' incomes.
   - **Institutional development:** NABARD helps strengthen rural financial institutions through training, capacity building, and technical assistance.
   - **Financial Inclusion:** NABARD is committed to promoting financial inclusion by improving access to credit and other financial services for rural and marginalized communities.
3. **NABARD's main initiatives:**

- **Rural Infrastructure Development Fund (RIDF):** Created to finance rural infrastructure projects such as roads, bridges, irrigation systems, and downspouts. The initiative aims to improve rural connectivity and support agricultural productivity.

- **Agricultural Sector Promotion Fund (FSPF):** Established to promote innovative and sustainable agricultural practices, including organic farming, integrated pest management, and climate-resilient agriculture.

- **Watershed Development Program:** Focuses on conserving soil and water resources through watershed management projects. The program aims to increase water availability, reduce soil erosion, and improve agricultural productivity.

- **Self-Help Group Banking Liaison Program:** Encourages the formation and funding of self-help groups to promote financial inclusion and the empowerment of rural women. The program has been successful in mobilizing savings and providing loans to many rural households.

Other major financial institutions

1. **Commercial banks:**
   - **Role: Commercial** banks are a major source of agricultural credit, providing short-, medium-- and

long-term loans to farmers for various agricultural activities.

- o **Initiatives:** Many commercial banks have their agricultural credit departments and offer specialized financial products for the agricultural sector. They also participate in government-sponsored programs such as Kisan Credit Card (KCC) and Pradhan Mantri Fasal Bima Yojana (PMFBY).

2. **Credit unions:**

- o **Role:** Co-operative banks operate at the village, district, and state levels, providing loans to farmers through co-operatives. They play an important role in the disbursement of loans in rural areas.

- o **Initiatives: Co-operative banks** offer a variety of lEnding products for agriculture and related activities, and participate in development and government programs to support farmers.

3. **Regional Rural Banks (RRBs):**

- o **Role:** RRBs are state-owned banks established to serve rural areas and provide loans to the agricultural sector. They aim to meet the financial needs of smallholder and smallholder farmers, agricultural workers, and rural artisans.

- o **Initiatives:** RRBs offer a range of financial products, including crop loans, equipment loans, and micro-irrigation and horticulture loans. They also participate in government programs such as the PM-Kisan and KCC programs.

4. **Microfinance Institutions (MFIs):**

   o **Role:** MFIs provide small loans to farmers and rural entrepreneurs, often through self-help groups (SHGs). They focus on financial inclusion and strengthening rural communities.

   o **Initiatives:** MFIs provide microcredit for agricultural inputs, livestock, and small equipment. They also provide financial literacy training and support for rural businesses.

5. **Non-Bank Financial Corporations (NBFCs):**

   o **Role:** NBFCs play an important role in lEnding to the agricultural sector, particularly in sectors that are not served by traditional banks. They offer flexible credit products and innovative financing solutions.

   o **Initiatives:** NBFCs provide equipment financing, working capital loans, and loans to agricultural businesses. They also offer financial products tailored to the needs of smallholders and smallholder farmers.

Influence of financial institutions on agricultural development

1. **Better access to credit:**

- NABARD-led financial institutions have significantly improved farmers' access to credit, allowing them to invest in modern farming practices, high-quality inputs, and infrastructure.

2. **Support for rural infrastructure:**
   - Programs like the RIDF have led to the development of critical rural infrastructure, including irrigation systems, roads, and storage facilities, resulting in increased agricultural productivity and market access.

3. **Promote sustainable practices:**
   - NABARD and other institutions have promoted sustainable agricultural practices through development programs and initiatives, helping farmers adopt climate-resilient and environmentally friEndly methods.

4. **Rural Community Empowerment:**
   - Initiatives such as the Mutual Aid Bank Liaison Programme have empowered rural communities, especially women, by providing access to credit, encouraging savings, and supporting income-generating activities.

In end, NABARD and other financial institutions play an important role in supporting agricultural financing and development in India. Their efforts have improved access to credit, supported rural infrastructure development, promoted sustainable practices, and strengthened rural communities, contributing to the growth and sustainability of the agricultural sector.

9.3: Crop Insurance

Crop insurance is an important component of agricultural financing, as it provides farmers with a safety net against the uncertainties and risks associated with farming. It helps stabilize farmers' incomes by compensating for crop losses due to various hazards, thus ensuring their economic security and stability.

Importance of crop insurance

- **Risk mitigation**: Crop insurance reduces farmers' financial risks related to natural disasters, pests, diseases, and market fluctuations.
- **Income Stabilization**: By compensating for crop losses, insurance helps stabilize farmers' incomes, allowing them to plan and invest for the next harvest season.
- **Credit Facility**: Insured crops make it easier for farmers to obtain loans from financial institutions because they reduce risk for lEnders.

Overview of Crop Insurance Systems in India

Many crop insurance policies in India aim to protect farmers from losses caused by unforeseen events. These systems are intEnded to cover various aspects of agricultural risks and provide comprehensive coverage.

Pradhan Mantri Fasal Bima Yojana (PMFBY)

- **Introduction**: The PMFBY was introduced in 2016 and is one of the largest crop insurance schemes in India.
- **Scope**: This includes all food and oilseed crops as well as annual cash and horticultural crops for which historical yield data is available.
- **Premium rate**: Farmers pay a nominal premium (2% for Kharif crops, 1.5% for rabi crops, and 5% for cash/horticultural crops), with the rest of the premium shared between the central government and the states.
- **Implementation**: The program is implemented by a network of insurance companies, banks, and government agencies to ensure comprehensive coverage and reach.
- **Benefits**: PMFBY offers comprehensive risk coverage from pre-sowing to post-harvest losses due to various natural and man-made hazards.

Weather-Based Crop Insurance Plans (WBCIS)

- **Introduction**: WBCIS aims to provide farmers with insurance coverage and financial support in the event of adverse weather conditions.

- **Mechanism**: The system uses weather parameters such as rainfall, temperature, humidity, and wind speed as triggers for insurance payments, rather than actual crop losses.
- **Benefits**: This approach allows for faster and more objective settlement of claims and shortens the time between claims and compensation.

Successful Implementation Case Studies

1. **Maharashtra**: In Maharashtra, the implementation of the PMFBY has helped farmers recover from severe drought conditions, allowing them to invest in subsequent harvest seasons.
2. **Rajasthan**: Weather-based crop insurance has proven to be particularly effective in Rajasthan, where erratic rainfall often leads to crop failures. The fast payment based on weather data has brought much-needed relief to farmers.
3. **Tamil Nadu**: The use of technology and mobile applications for the processing of applications under the PMFBY in Tamil Nadu has significantly reduced the time it takes to process applications and increased the efficiency of the system.

Challenges and solutions

- **Awareness and education**: Many farmers are still unaware of the benefits and procedures of crop insurance. It is important to raise awareness through education and awareness programs.

- **Claims Settlement**: Delays in the settlement of claims can undermine the benefits of crop insurance. Streamlining processes and using technology for quick assessments and payments can solve this problem.
- **Coverage gap**: There is a need to ensure that all farmers, including small and small farmers, have access to crop insurance. Expanding the scope of systems and simplifying registration processes can help close coverage gaps.

End

Crop insurance schemes such as PMFBY and WBCIS are important tools to secure farmers' livelihoods against the uncertainties of agriculture. By providing financial support under adverse conditions, these programs not only stabilize farmers' incomes but also contribute to the overall resilience and sustainability of the agricultural sector.

9.4: Risk Management in Agriculture

Farming is inherently risky because it depEnds on various uncontrollable factors such as weather, pests, diseases, and market conditions. Effective risk management is crucial to ensure the sustainability and profitability of agricultural operations. This explores the different types of risks in agriculture, strategies for dealing with these risks, and the role of government policies and technological innovations in risk management.

Introduction to Agricultural Risks

Agricultural risks can be divided into different types:

- **Production risks**: These include risks related to weather conditions (drought, floods, hail), pests, diseases, and the quality of inputs (seeds, fertilizers).
- Fluctuations in market prices, changes in supply and demand, and international trade policies can have a significant impact on farmers' incomes.
- **Financial risks**: These include uncertainties regarding credit availability, interest rates, and creditworthiness.
- **Institutional risks**: Changes in government policies, regulations, and assistance programs can impact farms and profitability.

Risk Management Strategies

Farmers use a variety of strategies to manage and mitigate the risks associated with farming. These strategies include diversification, hedging, and insurance.

diversity

- **Crop diversification**: Growing a variety of crops reduces reliance on a single crop and increases the risk of failure.

For example, farmers can grow a mixture of grains, legumes, and vegetables.

- **Income diversification**: Engaging in multiple income-generating activities, such as animal husbandry, agricultural processing, and off-farm employment, can provide additional financial stability.

Blanket

- **Futures**: Farmers can use futures contracts to lock in the prices of their crops, protecting themselves from price fluctuations. This is especially useful for cash crops such as cotton and sugarcane.
- **Futures**: Similar to futures, futures contracts involve agreements between farmers and buyers to sell a certain amount of produce at a predetermined price.

Shield

- **Crop Insurance**: As discussed on the previous , crop insurance plans such as the PMFBY provide financial compensation for crop losses due to various hazards.
- **Livestock insurance**: Livestock insurance protects farmers against losses due to disease, theft, or natural disasters that affect their animals.

Government Policies and Programs

The government plays an important role in supporting risk management in agriculture through a variety of policies and programs.

- **Subsidy and support programs**: Government subsidies for inputs such as seeds, fertilizers, and irrigation can help reduce production risks. Support schemes such as minimum support prices (MSPs) ensure price stability for certain crops.
- Credit facilities: Accessible and affordable credit through institutional sources such as banks and cooperatives can reduce financial risks. Programs such as the Kisan Credit Card (KCC) offer flexible credit facilities to farmers.
- **Advisory Services**: Agricultural Advisory Services provide farmers with the knowledge and skills to implement risk management practices. These services provide training on new technologies, pest and disease management, and market trEnds.

Technological innovation in risk management

Technological advances have significantly improved farmers' ability to manage risk more effectively.

- **Weather forecasting**: Accurate weather forecasts allow farmers to make informed decisions about planting, irrigation, and harvesting, reducing the impact of adverse weather conditions.

- **Mobile apps**: Various mobile apps provide real-time information on weather, market prices, and best farming practices, helping farmers better manage risk.
- **Precision agriculture**: Technologies such as GPS, remote sensing, and IoT devices enable precision agriculture, optimizing the use of resources and reducing the risks associated with agricultural production.
- **Blockchain technology**: Blockchain can improve the transparency and traceability of agricultural supply chains, reduce market risks, and ensure fair transactions.

End

Effective risk management in agriculture is important to ensure the sustainability and profitability of farms. By using a combination of diversification, hedging, and insurance strategies supported by government policies and technological innovations, farmers can better manage the uncertainties of agriculture. These measures not only protect farmers' livelihoods but also contribute to the overall resilience and sustainability of the agricultural sector.

9.5: Recent developments in the field of agricultural financing

The agricultural finance landscape in India has changed significantly in recent years, driven by technological advancements, innovative financial products, and supportive government policies. These developments aim to increase financial inclusion, improve access to credit, and promote sustainable agricultural practices. This looks at current trEnds and innovations in agricultural finance, their impact on agriculture, and future opportunities.

Digital Finance and Fintech in Agriculture

Digital finance and financial technology (fintech) have changed the way farmers access financial services. These technologies offer convenient, efficient, and cost-effective solutions for managing financial transactions and accessing credit.

- **Mobile banking**: Mobile banking platforms allow farmers to conduct banking transactions through their mobile phones and provide easy access to savings, loans, and payments without the need for physical bank branches.
- **Digital payment system**: Digital payment systems such as the Unified Payment Interface (UPI), e-wallets, and Aadhaar-enabled payment services have simplified transactions and made it easier for farmers to receive payments for their products and pay for their inputs.
- **Digital lEnding platforms**: FinTech companies offer digital lEnding platforms that assess farmers' creditworthiness based on alternative data sources such as mobile usage patterns and transaction history, providing quick and easy access to credit.

Blockchain technology for transparent transactions

Blockchain technology offers a secure and transparent way to manage transactions and supply chains in agriculture. It helps build trust and reduce fraud by providing an immutable record of transactions.

- **Smart contracts**: Blockchain-based smart contracts automatically execute transactions when predefined conditions are met to ensure on-time payments and reduce disputes.
- **Traceability**: Blockchain makes it possible to search for agricultural products from farm to fork while ensuring quality and authenticity, which can improve farmers' access to the market and get better prices.

Recent policy changes and their impact

Government policy plays an important role in shaping the agricultural finance landscape. Recent policy changes aim to improve access to credit, support financial inclusion, and promote sustainable practices.

- **Kisan Credit Card (KCC) Reforms:** The government has simplified the KCC application process, making it easier for farmers to obtain short-term loans for cultivation and related activities.
- **Interest Subsidy Program**: The Interest Subsidy Program provides farmers with a preferential interest rate on loans,

reduces their financial burden, and encourages investment in agriculture.

- **Agricultural Infrastructure Fund (AIF):** Launched in 2020, the AIF provides medium- and long-term debt financing for projects related to post-harvest management and infrastructure development, boosting value creation and reducing post-harvest losses.

Mobile Banking & Digital Payment Systems

The introduction of mobile banking and digital payment systems has revolutionized financial transactions in rural areas and brought several benefits to agriculture.

- **Easy access**: Mobile banking apps and digital wallets provide farmers with 24-hour access to financial services, reducing reliance on physical bank branches.
- **Transaction efficiency**: Digital payment systems enable fast and secure transactions, reducing the time and effort required for financial transactions.
- **Financial inclusion**: These systems promote financial inclusion by providing banking services to the unbanked or unbanked population in remote areas.

Future TrEnds and Opportunities

With continued advances in technology and supportive government initiatives, the future of agricultural finance looks bright. Many trEnds and opportunities are likely to shape this sector in the coming years.

- **Agritech startups**: Agritech startups develop innovative solutions for access to credit, insurance, and market connections, improving the overall efficiency of the agricultural value chain.
- **Big data and AI**: Big data analytics and artificial intelligence (AI) can provide insights into plant health, soil conditions, and market trEnds, helping farmers make informed financial decisions.
- **Sustainable finance**: Sustainable finance is highlighted with financial products designed to promote environmentally friEndly practices such as organic farming, the use of renewable energy, and water conservation.

End

Recent developments in agricultural finance have significantly improved access to credit, improved financial inclusion, and promoted sustainable agricultural practices. Innovations in digital finance, blockchain technology, and supportive government policies have provided farmers with better financial tools and services. As technology evolves and new opportunities emerge, the agricultural finance sector is poised to play a key role in transforming Indian agriculture and ensuring its sustainability and resilience.

Chapter 10: Agricultural Research and Education

10.1: Importance of Agricultural Research

Agricultural research plays an important role in increasing the productivity and sustainability of agriculture. In a country like India, where agriculture is the backbone of the economy, the importance of research cannot be overstated. Through rigorous scientific research and innovation, new farming techniques, plant varieties, and farming methods are being developed to ensure food security and economic sustainability.

Important contributions of agricultural research

1. Improved plant varieties

One of the main contributions of agricultural research is the development of improved plant varieties. These varieties are bred for high yields, improved nutrient quality, disease resistance, and adaptability to different climatic conditions. For example, the introduction of high-yielding varieties (HYVs) during the Green Revolution gave a major boost to food production in India.

2. Pest and Disease Management

The research has led to the development of integrated pest management (IPM) practices that reduce the use of harmful pesticides while effectively controlling pests. It not only protects the plants but also ensures the protection of the environment and human health.

3. Soil and water management

Agricultural research has led to the emergence of innovative soil and water management techniques that have helped farmers use resources more efficiently. Practices such as precision agriculture, drip irrigation, and soil health monitoring improve water-use efficiency and maintain soil fertility.

4. Climate resilience

With climate change posing a significant threat to agriculture, research is essential for the development of climate-resilient crops and agricultural practices. These innovations help mitigate the negative effects of climate change while ensuring stable agricultural productivity.

5. Sustainable agricultural practices

Agricultural research promotes sustainable agricultural practices that increase productivity without depleting natural resources. Techniques such as conservation agriculture, organic farming, and agroforestry are the result of extensive research efforts to find a balance between agriculture and environmental protection.

Economic impact

1. Increase farmers' incomes

Research-driven innovations lead to higher agricultural productivity, which directly translates into higher incomes for farmers. Improved cultivars and farming techniques allow farmers to obtain better yields and quality products, which in turn leads to better prices in the market.

2. Food safety

Agricultural research ensures food security by developing plant varieties that are resistant to pests, diseases, and climate change. This stability in food production helps maintain a constant food supply and reduces the risk of food shortages.

3. Rural development

Advances in agriculture through research stimulate rural development. Increasing agricultural productivity leads to the development of agricultural industries, creates employment opportunities, and improves the quality of life in rural areas.

Social and environmental benefits

1. Environmental protection

Sustainable agricultural practices developed through research reduce the environmental footprint of agriculture. Techniques such as reduced tillage, organic farming, and integrated pest management help to preserve biodiversity and protect natural resources.

2. Health and nutrition

Research contributes to the development of biofortified plants that fill the nutritional gaps of the population. Plants rich in essential vitamins and minerals play an important role in combating malnutrition and improving public health.

3. Empowering farmers

Access to research and new technologies gives farmers the knowledge and tools they need to improve their farming practices. Advisory services play an important role in disseminating this knowledge and ensuring that the benefits of research reach the grassroots.

After all, agricultural research is the cornerstone of modern agriculture, driving progress that leads to increased productivity, sustainability, and resilience. It supports economic growth, ensures food security, promotes environmental protection, and improves farmers' livelihoods. Going forward, continued investments in agricultural research and innovation will be key to meeting the new challenges in the agricultural sector.

10.2: Major Research Institutes in India

India has a strong network of agricultural research institutes dedicated to promoting the country's agricultural sector. These institutions play an important role in developing new technologies, improving plant varieties, and promoting sustainable agricultural practices. Here we highlight some of India's leading research institutions that have made significant contributions to agricultural research and education.

1. Indian Council for Agricultural Research (ICAR)

Bird's eye view

The Indian Council of Agricultural Research (ICAR) is the supreme body responsible for coordinating, directing, and managing agricultural research and education in India. The ICAR was founded in 1929 and is under the authority of the Ministry of Agriculture and Farmers' Welfare.

Significant contributions

- **Improving harvesting**: ICAR has developed several high-yielding, disease-resistant plant varieties that have significantly increased agricultural productivity.
- **Livestock:** The Council made progress in the areas of livestock, health, and nutrition, contributing to the growth of the dairy and poultry sectors.

- **Fisheries and aquaculture**: ICAR has promoted sustainable fishing and aquaculture practices, increased fish production, and improved livelihoods in coastal areas.

2. International Plant Research Institute for the Semi-Arid Tropics (ICRISAT)

Bird's eye view

ICRISAT is an international organization headquartered in Hyderabad dedicated to improving the livelihoods of poor farmers in the semi-arid tropics through agricultural research for development.

Significant contributions

- **Crop resilience**: ICRISAT has developed drought and climate-tolerant plant varieties specifically for Jowar, Bajra, Gram, and groundnut.
- **Soil health**: The institute promotes sustainable soil management practices, and improves soil fertility and productivity.
- **Water conservation**: ICRISAT focuses on water-efficient technologies and watershed management to address water scarcity in semi-arid regions.

3. National Dairy Research Institute (NDRI)

Bird's eye view

Based in Karnal, Haryana, NDRI is one of India's leading institutes dedicated to dairy research. It is affiliated with ICAR and focuses on improving milk production, processing, and farming.

Significant contributions

- **Genetic improvement**: NDRI has made significant progress in dairy farming, which has led to an increase in milk production and quality.
- **Dairy technology**: The institute develops innovative milk processing technologies that ensure better quality and longer shelf life of dairy products.
- **Training and education**: NDRI offers comprehensive training programs for dairy farmers and professionals who promote best practices in milk management.

4. Central Marine Fisheries Research Institute (CMFRI)

Bird's eye view

Based in Kochi, Kerala, CMFRI focuses on marine fisheries research and management. It operates under the ICAR and plays an important role in the sustainable development of marine fisheries.

Significant contributions

- **Marine biodiversity**: The CMFRI conducts extensive research on marine biodiversity, which contributes to the conservation of marine ecosystems.

- **Fisheries Management**: The Institute develops sustainable fishing practices and management strategies to ensure the long-term sustainability of marine resources.
- **Aquaculture**: The CMFRI promotes sustainable aquaculture practices, increases fish production, and supports coastal communities.

5. Indian Agricultural Research Institute (IARI)

Bird's eye view

IARI, based in New Delhi, is India's leading agricultural research, education, and advisory institute. Known as the "Pusa Institute", IARI plays a key role in the green revolution and promotes agricultural innovation.

Significant contributions

- **Plant research**: IARI has developed several high-yielding, disease-resistant plant varieties, particularly for wheat, rice, and pulses.
- **Soil Science**: The institute conducts cutting-edge research in soil science, and promotes soil health and sustainable agricultural practices.
- **Post-harvest technology**: IARI focuses on improving post-harvest management and processing techniques, reducing food losses, and improving food security.

6. Central Institute of Agricultural Engineering (CIAE)

Bird's eye view

Based in Bhopal, Madhya Pradesh, the CIAE focuses on research and development in agricultural engineering. The institute aims to mechanize Indian agriculture and improve agricultural efficiency.

Significant contributions

- **Agricultural machinery**: CIAE develops innovative agricultural machinery and equipment, increases agricultural productivity, and reduces labor costs.
- **Energy management**: The institute promotes renewable energy solutions and the efficient use of energy in agriculture.
- **Irrigation Technology**: CIAE advances irrigation technologies and improves water use efficiency and crop yields.

7. Central Research Institute for Cotton Technology (CIRCUIT)

Bird's eye view

CIRCET, based in Mumbai, specializes in cotton research and technology development. It operates under the umbrella of ICAR and aims to improve the quality and value of cotton products.

Significant contributions

- **Fiber Quality**: CIRCOT focuses on improving the quality of cotton fibers to make Indian cotton competitive in global markets.
- **Processing Technology**: The institute develops efficient cotton processing technologies and improves cotton products.
- **Use of by-products**: CIRCOT studies the use of cotton by-products, thus promoting sustainable and profitable cotton cultivation.

End

India's agricultural research institutes play an important role in advancing agricultural practices, food security, and promoting sustainable development. His contributions include crop improvement, animal husbandry, fisheries, dairy technology, and agricultural engineering. With additional investment and support from these institutions, India can address the challenges of the agricultural sector and drive future growth and innovation.

10.3: Extension Services and Their Role

Extension services play an important role in bridging the gap between agricultural research and its practical application in the field. These services are designed to transfer knowledge and technologies from research institutes to farmers and ensure that the latest advances in agriculture are applied effectively to increase productivity, sustainability, and profitability.

Agricultural extension concept

Agricultural extension refers to the distribution of information, technology, and services to farmers and other actors in the agricultural sector. The main objective is to improve agricultural practices, increase yields, and improve the livelihoods of farming communities. Consulting services include a wide range of activities, including education, training, demonstration, consulting services, and support for the adoption of new technologies.

Key features of extension services

1. Dissemination of knowledge

Advisory services are essential for disseminating the latest research, innovations, and best practices to farmers. It includes information on improved plant varieties, pest and disease management, soil health, water conservation, and sustainable agricultural practices.

2. Capacity building

Education and training programs run by advisory services improve farmers' skills and knowledge. These programs cover various aspects of agriculture, such as crop production, livestock, post-harvest processing, and farm management. Capacity building enables farmers to adopt modern farming techniques and improve their productivity.

3. Consulting services

Consultants provide farmers with customized advisory services that meet their specific needs and challenges. This includes site visits, consultations, and technical support. Advisory services help farmers make informed decisions about crop selection, pest management, fertilization, irrigation, and other important aspects of agriculture.

4. Demonstration projects

Demonstration projects are practical implementations of new technologies and practices on a small scale to demonstrate their benefits. These projects allow farmers to see first-hand the benefits of adopting new methods and encourage them to implement these practices on their farms.

5. Connecting farmers to markets

Advisory services facilitate relationships between farmers and markets, enabling them to obtain better market information, negotiate fair prices, and reduce post-harvest losses. This includes organizing farmers' markets, promoting contract farming, and supporting value-added and processing initiatives.

Top Consulting Service Providers in India

1. Krishi Vigyan KEndras (KVK)

KVKs are district-level agricultural advisory centers established by ICAR. They are the main source of advisory services, providing training, demonstrations, and advisory services to farmers.

2. State Agricultural University (SAU)

UAS plays an important role in agricultural extension by conducting research and providing education, and advisory services. They work with KVK and other institutions to pass on knowledge and technology to farmers. The SAU also organizes fairs, exhibitions, and training programs for farmers.

3. National Agricultural Extension Management Institute (MANAGE)

Based in Hyderabad, MANAGE is a leading organization that provides training and capacity-building programs for consulting staff. The aim is to improve the effectiveness of agricultural extension services through training, research, and advice.

4. Agricultural Technology Management Agency (ATMA)

ATMA is a government initiative that aims to promote decentralized and on-demand advisory services. It works at the district level and integrates various stakeholders such as farmers, research institutes, and government agencies to conduct advisory activities based on local needs.

Challenges and solutions in extension services

1. Restricted access and accessibility

Many farmers, especially in remote areas, have limited access to advisory services. It restricts the dissemination of knowledge and technologies.

Solution:

- **Digital advisory services:** Leveraging mobile, internet, and social media platforms to provide information and advisory services to a wider audience.
- **Farmer Field Schools:** Establish field schools where farmers can learn through hands-on experience.

2. Insufficient training of advisors

Consultants may not have the skills and knowledge to effectively transfer technology and provide consulting services.

Solution:

- **Capacity Building Programs:** Continuous training and development programs to advise staff to improve their technical and communication skills.
- **Partnership with Research Institutions:** Collaborate with research institutions to keep advisors informed of the latest developments in agriculture.

3. Resistance to change

Farmers may be reluctant to adopt new technologies and practices due to traditional beliefs, lack of awareness, or fear of risk.

Solution:

- **Demonstration projects:** Implementation of demonstration projects to demonstrate the benefits of new technologies and practices.
- **Peer learning:** Encourage farmers who have successfully introduced new methods to share their experiences with their peers.

End

Advisory services are essential for the growth and development of agriculture. They ensure that the benefits of agricultural research reach the grassroots and give farmers the knowledge and tools they need to improve their productivity and livelihoods. By addressing challenges and leveraging innovative solutions, advisory services can significantly increase the impact of agricultural research and contribute to sustainable agricultural development in India.

10.4: Agricultural Education and Training

Agricultural education and training are fundamental elements of a prosperous agricultural sector. They equip individuals with the knowledge, skills, and competencies to meet the challenges of modern agriculture, increase productivity, and promote sustainable agricultural practices. In India, various institutions and programs play an important role in promoting agricultural education and training.

Importance of agricultural education

1. Knowledge Enhancement

Agricultural education provides a comprehensive understanding of various aspects of agriculture, including plant science, soil health, pest management, agricultural economics, and agricultural engineering. This knowledge enables individuals to make informed decisions and implement best practices.

2. Skills Development

Practical training and practical experience are an integral part of agricultural training. These elements enable individuals to acquire the skills necessary to apply theoretical knowledge in real-world agricultural situations and to increase their effectiveness and efficiency.

3. Innovation and research

Educational institutions are centers of innovation and research. They foster a culture of research and experimentation that leads to the development of new technologies, new plant varieties, and new agricultural practices that drive agricultural progress.

4. Accountability and Leadership

Agricultural education gives individuals the tools and confidence to lead in their communities. Farmers and educated professionals can advocate for better agricultural policies, adopt innovative practices, and mentor others.

Important Institutions in Agricultural Education

1. State Agricultural University (SAU)

UACs are important for providing higher education in agriculture. They offer undergraduate, postgraduate, and doctoral programs in various agricultural disciplines. The UAA is also engaged in research and advisory activities to bridge the gap between education and practical farming.

- **Examples:** Punjab Agricultural University (PAU), Tamil Nadu Agricultural University (TNAU), and Acharya N.G. Ranga Agricultural University (ANGRAU) are known for their contributions to agricultural education and research.

2. Indian Council for Agricultural Research (ICAR)

The RAC plays a dual role in agricultural research and education. She supervises and supports many universities and agricultural research institutes across India. ICAR also develops curricula, organizes examinations, and grants accreditations to agricultural institutions.

- **Example:** The ICAR-National Academy of Agricultural Research Management (NAARM) offers advanced training programs for agronomists, teachers, and administrative staff.

3. College of Agriculture

These colleges are affiliated with various universities and focus on basic and postgraduate education in agriculture. They offer specialized programs in agronomy, horticulture, animal husbandry, agricultural engineering, etc.

- **Examples:** The Pune Agricultural College, headed by Mahatma Phule Krishi Vidyapeeth, and the Vellayani Agricultural College, under the umbrella of the Kerala Agricultural University, are notable institutions.

4. Krishi Vigyan KEndras (KVK)

KVKs play an important role in providing vocational training and capacity-building programs to farmers, rural youth, and counseling workers. They conduct tests, demonstrations, and short courses on the farm to encourage the adoption of new technologies.

- **Example:** The KVKs work under the auspices of ICAR and are spread across all districts of India and act as local centers for agricultural education and training.

Training Programs and Initiatives

1. Training program for farmers

These programs are designed to improve farmers' skills and knowledge and enable them to adopt modern farming practices. Topics include crop management, pest management, soil health, water conservation, and post-harvest management.

- **Example:** Training programs for farmers managed by KVKs and UAS offer practical training and practical demonstrations.

2. Professional training

Vocational training programs are aimed at young people and women in rural areas and offer courses in areas such as dairy farming, poultry farming, organic farming, agricultural processing, and the agricultural industry. These programs aim to create employment opportunities and promote entrepreneurship in the agricultural sector.

- **Example:** Rural IndepEndent Employment Training Institutes (RSETI) provide vocational training in agriculture and related activities.

3. Capacity building for consultants

Training programs for consultants are focused on improving their technical knowledge and communication skills. This allows them to effectively share information and technology with farmers.

- **Example:** The National Agricultural Extension Management Institute (MANAGE) offers specialized training programs for advisory staff.

4. Digital and online training

With the advent of digital technologies, online training programs and online learning platforms have gained traction. These platforms provide flexible and accessible learning opportunities for farmers and agricultural professionals.

- **Example:** The eNAM platform offers online training modules on market access and agricultural marketing. The ICAR online course platform offers digital learning resources on various agricultural topics.

Challenges and solutions in agricultural education and training

1. Accessibility and inclusivity

Access to quality agricultural education and training may be limited, especially in remote and underserved areas. Ensuring inclusion is essential to the widespread adoption of modern agricultural practices.

Solution:

- **Satellite and distance learning:** Using satellite communications and internet connectivity to deliver education and training in remote areas.
- **Scholarships and Financial Aid:** Provide scholarships and financial assistance to students from marginalized communities to promote inclusion in agricultural education.

2. Relevance of the curriculum

The agricultural education curriculum should be updated regularly to reflect the latest advances in agricultural science and technology.

Solution:

- **Industry-academia collaboration:** Strengthen partnerships between academic institutions and agribusiness to ensure programs are relevant and up-to-date.
- **Ongoing Curriculum Review:** Establish mechanisms for regular review and updating of curricula based on emerging trEnds and research findings.

3. Hands-on training

While theoretical knowledge is essential, practical training is important for effective teaching and application in agriculture.

Solution:

- **Experiential learning:** Integrate experiential learning opportunities such as internships, field trips, and on-farm training into the curriculum.
- **Simulations and models:** The use of simulation tools and models to provide hands-on experience in a controlled environment.

End

Agricultural education and training are the cornerstones of a resilient and progressive agricultural sector. By equipping individuals with the necessary knowledge, skills, and competencies, these programs foster innovation, increase productivity, and promote sustainable agricultural practices. Continuous investment and improvement in agricultural education and training are critical for the future of agriculture in India.

10.5: Innovations and Future TrEnds in Agriculture

Agriculture is constantly evolving, driven by technological advances and innovative practices that meet the challenges of modern agriculture. As the world's population grows and the effects of climate change become more evident, the need for sustainable and efficient agricultural practices becomes more important than ever. This highlights some of the key innovations and future trEnds that are shaping the future of agriculture in India and around the world.

Technological innovations

1. Precision Agriculture

Precision farming involves the use of advanced technologies to monitor and control agricultural production with high accuracy. This approach optimizes the use of resources and improves crop yields.

- **GPS and GIS:** Global Positioning System (GPS) and Geographic Information System (GIS) enable accurate mapping and monitoring of farms, allowing farmers to more effectively apply inputs such as water, fertilizers, and pesticides.
- **Drones**: Drones equipped with sensors and cameras provide real-time data on plant health, soil conditions, and pest infestations, helping farmers make informed decisions.
- **IoT and sensors**: The Internet of Things (IoT) and sensor technology monitor environmental conditions, soil moisture, and plant health, facilitating rapid response and reducing waste.

2. Biotechnology and genetic engineering

Biotechnology and genetic engineering have revolutionized agriculture by developing crops with advanced properties such as pest resistance, drought tolerance, and better nutrient content.

- **Genetically modified organisms (GMOs):** GMOs are modified to have desirable properties, resulting in higher yields and less reliance on chemical inputs.
- **CRISPR-Cas9**: This gene-editing technique allows precise modifications of the plant's genome, thus allowing the development of crops with specific beneficial characteristics.

3. Vertical farming and hydroponics

Vertical farming and hydroponics offer innovative solutions for growing in controlled environments that lead to efficient use of space and resources.

- **Vertical farming**: This method involves growing crops in vertical layers, often in urban settings, using controlled environments to optimize growing conditions.
- **Hydroponics**: Hydroponic systems grow plants without soil with a nutrient-rich water solution. This technology saves water and can be used in areas with poor soil quality.

4. Robotics and automation

Robotics and automation technologies are transforming labor-intensive farms, improving efficiency and reducing costs.

- **Autonomous tractors and machines**: Autonomous tractors and machines perform tasks such as planting, mowing, and weeding with precision, reducing the need for manual labor.

- **Harvesting robots**: These robots can identify and select ripe fruits and vegetables, increasing harvesting efficiency and reducing waste.

Ongoing practice

1. Conservation agriculture

Conservation agriculture promotes sustainable agricultural practices that protect soil health and increase biodiversity.

- **No-till farming:** This practice involves minimal soil disturbance, reduced erosion, and improved soil structure.
- **Cover cropping:** Off-season cover cropping protects the soil from erosion, increases soil fertility, and suppresses weeds.

2. Agricultural Sciences

Agroecology integrates ecological principles into agricultural practice, thus promoting biodiversity and sustainability.

- **Polyculture**: Growing multiple plant species in the same area improves soil health and reduces pest pressure.
- **Agroforestry**: Integrating trees and shrubs into agricultural landscapes increases biodiversity, improves soil health, and provides additional sources of income.

3. Organic farming

Organic farming avoids synthetic chemicals and emphasizes natural processes to maintain soil health and produce nutritious food.

- **Natural Pest Control**: The use of natural enemies and biopesticides for pest control reduces the use of chemicals and promotes ecosystem health.
- **Compost and manure**: Organic farming relies on manure and animal manure to enrich soil fertility, and increase microbial activity and nutrient availability.

Future trEnds

1. Climate-smart agriculture

Climate-smart agriculture aims to increase productivity and resilience to climate change while reducing greenhouse gas emissions.

- **Drought-tolerant crops**: The development and propagation of crops that can withstand water scarcity ensures stable yields under changing climatic conditions.
- **Water-efficient irrigation**: The use of techniques such as drip irrigation and sprinkler irrigation optimizes water use, reducing the effects of droughts.

2. Digital agriculture

Digital agriculture uses data analytics, artificial intelligence (AI), and machine learning to optimize farming practices.

- **Farm management software**: Digital tools help farmers plan, monitor, and manage their farms more efficiently.
- **Big data and analytics**: The analysis of large data sets enables predictive modeling and decision-making, improving agricultural productivity and sustainability.

3. Urban agriculture

Urban agriculture responds to the challenges of food security and sustainability in urban areas by producing locally.

- **Roof garden**: Using the roof area for gardening increases green space and provides fresh produce.
- **Community gardens**: Shared garden spaces in urban areas encourage community engagement and provide access to fresh, locally grown food.

4. Alternative proteins

The demand for sustainable protein sources is driving innovation in alternative proteins and reducing reliance on traditional livestock farming.

- **Plant-based proteins**: The development of protein-rich foods from plants reduces the environmental impact of meat production.

- **Cultured meat**: Lab-grown meat offers a sustainable alternative to traditional meat with fewer resources and fewer greenhouse gas emissions.

End

The future of agriculture lies in the integration of innovative technologies and sustainable practices that meet the challenges of modern agriculture. By embracing advancements such as precision agriculture, biotechnology, and digital tools, as well as promoting sustainable practices such as conservation agriculture and agroecology, the agricultural sector can increase productivity, ensure food security, and reduce environmental impacts. Continued investments in research and education will be key to driving these innovations and ensuring a sustainable and prosperous future for agriculture.

References

Chapter 1: Introduction to Indian Agriculture

1. Bhalla, G. S., & Singh, G. (2001). *Indian agriculture: Four decades of development.* Sage Publications.

2. Chand, R., & Raju, S. S. (2009). Agricultural policy and performance in India. *Economic and Political Weekly, 44*(52), 16-18.

3. Chand, R., & Raju, S. S. (2009). Agricultural policy and performance in India. *Economic and Political Weekly, 44*(52), 16-18.

4. Government of India. (2020). *Indian agriculture: Performance and challenges.* Ministry of Agriculture and Farmers Welfare.

5. Kumar, P., & Mittal, S. (2006). Agricultural productivity trEnds in India: Sustainability issues. *Agricultural Economics Research Review, 19*(2), 71-88.

6. Rao, C. H. H. (2003). *Agricultural growth, rural poverty, and environmental degradation in India.* Oxford University Press.

Chapter 2: Agro-Climatic Zones of India

1. ICAR. (2014). *Handbook of agriculture.* Indian Council of Agricultural Research.

2. Ravindra, A., & Kaur, P. (2015). Impact of climate change on agricultural productivity in India. *Journal of Agrometeorology, 17*(2), 141-145.

3. Sehgal, J. (1990). *Agro-ecological regions of India.* National Bureau of Soil Survey and Land Use Planning.

4. Singh, S., & Mukherjee, J. (2008). Agro-climatic zones and agricultural potential in India. *Asian Journal of Agriculture and Development, 5*(2), 35-50.

5. Venkateswarlu, B., & Shanker, A. K. (2009). Climate change and agriculture over India. *Climate Change and Crops*, 45-64.

Chapter 3: Soil and Water Management

1. Bhattacharyya, T., Pal, D. K., & Mandal, C. (2013). *Soils of India*. National Bureau of Soil Survey and Land Use Planning.

2. GOI. (2019). *Pradhan Mantri Krishi Sinchai Yojana (PMKSY) Guidelines*. Ministry of Agriculture and Farmers Welfare.

3. Hillel, D. (2000). *Salinity management for sustainable irrigation: Integrating science, environment, and economics*. World Bank Publications.

4. Shah, T., et al. (2009). *India's groundwater irrigation economy: The challenge of balancing livelihoods and environmental sustainability*. International Water Management Institute.

5. Tyagi, N. K., Sharma, D. K., & Lohan, S. K. (2014). Water management strategies for sustainable agriculture in arid regions. *Water Resources Management, 28*(3), 857-875.

Chapter 4: Crop Production and Management

1. Balasubramanian, V., & Hill, J. E. (2002). Direct seeding of rice in Asia: Emerging issues and strategic research needs for the 21st century. *Direct Seeding: Research Issues and Opportunities*, 15-42.

2. GOI. (2021). *National mission for sustainable agriculture*. Ministry of Agriculture and Farmers Welfare.

3. Hegde, N. G. (2010). Sustainable agriculture in India. *International Journal of Sustainable Development and World Ecology, 17*(4), 231-238.

4. Lal, R., & Stewart, B. A. (2013). *Principles of sustainable soil management in agroecosystems.* CRC Press.

5. Swaminathan, M. S. (2000). *From green revolution to evergreen revolution: Pathways and paradigms for sustainable agriculture in India.* M.S. Swaminathan Research Foundation.

Chapter 5: Horticulture and Plantation Crops

1. Bose, T. K., & Som, M. G. (1986). *Vegetables in India.* Naya Prokash.

2. Chadha, K. L., & Pareek, O. P. (1993). *Advances in horticulture (Vol. 3): Fruit crops.* Malhotra Publishing House.

3. Kumar, N. (2016). *Introduction to horticulture.* Oxford Book Company.

4. Ravi, S. (2015). Post-harvest management of horticultural crops. *Journal of Horticulture, 22*(3), 250-260.

5. Thompson, A. K. (2003). *Postharvest technology of fruit and vegetables.* Blackwell Publishing.

Chapter 6: Livestock and Poultry Management

1. Banerjee, G. C. (2008). *A textbook of animal husbandry.* Oxford & IBH Publishing.

2. De, U. K. (2012). *Economics of livestock in India.* New Century Publications.

3. GOI. (2018). *National livestock mission guidelines.* Ministry of Agriculture and Farmers Welfare.

4. Misra, R., & Misra, S. K. (2003). Dairy farming in India: Problems and prospects. *Asian Journal of Dairy and Food Research, 22*(1), 1-7.

5. National Dairy Development Board. (2020). *Annual report.* NDDB.

Chapter 7: Fisheries and Aquaculture

1. Ayyappan, S., & Krishnan, M. (2004). Fisheries sector in India: Dimensions of development. *Indian Journal of Agricultural Economics, 59*(3), 391-412.

2. GOI. (2020). *Pradhan Mantri Matsya Sampada Yojana (PMMSY) guidelines.* Ministry of Fisheries, Animal Husbandry, and Dairying.

3. Handbook of Fisheries and Aquaculture. (2006). *Indian Council of Agricultural Research.* ICAR.

4. Jhingran, V. G. (1991). *Fish and fisheries of India.* Hindustan Publishing Corporation.

5. Pillay, T. V. R., & Kutty, M. N. (2005). *Aquaculture: Principles and practices.* Blackwell Publishing.

Chapter 8: Agricultural Marketing and Trade

1. Acharya, S. S., & Agarwal, N. L. (2004). *Agricultural marketing in India.* Oxford & IBH Publishing.

2. GOI. (2016). *National agriculture market (eNAM) guidelines.* Ministry of Agriculture and Farmers Welfare.

3. Kumar, A., & Sharma, P. (2013). Agriculture marketing reforms in India: An analysis of competition and efficiency effects. *Journal of Agricultural Economics Research Review, 26*(1), 73-80.

4. Mittal, S. (2007). Strengthening backward and forward linkages in horticulture: Some successful initiatives. *Agricultural Economics Research Review, 20*(1), 457-475.

5. Saxena, R. (2018). *Marketing management of agricultural products.* Prentice Hall India Learning Private Limited.

Chapter 9: Agricultural Finance and Insurance

1. Bhalla, G. S., & Singh, G. (2010). *Farmers' access to credit and insurance in India*. Sage Publications.

2. GOI. (2018). *Pradhan Mantri Fasal Bima Yojana (PMFBY) guidelines*. Ministry of Agriculture and Farmers Welfare.

3. Mahajan, V. (2013). *Agricultural finance in India: The role of NABARD*. Sage Publications.

4. NABARD. (2021). *Annual report*. National Bank for Agriculture and Rural Development.

5. Ray, S. K. (2008). Agricultural finance in India: The state of the art. *Indian Journal of Agricultural Economics, 63*(1), 1-18.

Chapter 10: Agricultural Research and Education

1. Birner, R., & Anderson, J. R. (2007). How to make agricultural extension demand-driven? The case of India's agricultural extension policy. *IFPRI Discussion Paper 00729*.

2. Evenson, R. E., & Jha, D. (1973). The contribution of agricultural research system to agricultural production in India. *Indian Journal of Agricultural Economics, 28*(4), 11-34.

3. ICAR. (2019). *Handbook of agriculture*. Indian Council of Agricultural Research.

4. Pal, S., & Joshi, P. K. (2008). Agricultural research and extension in India: Institutional structure and investments. *Indian Journal of Agricultural Economics, 63*(1), 1-19.

5. Swaminathan, M. S. (1998). *The quest for food security: Policies and technologies*. M.S. Swaminathan Research Foundation.